CW01514417

*Frontispiece*

At the command of the *mahawat*, Kathleen uses her trunk to throw showers of water over her head while Daisy looks on.

# TEN THOUSAND MILES
## ON ELEPHANTS

# TEN THOUSAND MILES
## ON
# ELEPHANTS

By OLIVE SMYTHIES

*Author of "Jungle Lady"*

*With a Foreword by*

LORD HAILEY
P.C. G.C.S.I. G.C.M.G. G.C.I.E.

**NATRAJ PUBLISHERS**
Dehra Dun

Text copyright © Natraj Publishers

First Published 1961
Reprinted 2007

ISBN: 978-81-8158-101-3

All rights reserved. This book is sold subject to the condition that it shall not, by way of trade or otherwise, be lent, resold, hired out, or otherwise circulated without the publisher's prior written consent in any form of binding or cover other than that in which it is published and without a similar condition including this condition being imposed on the subsequent purchaser and without limiting the rights under copyright reserved above, no part of this publication may be reproduced, stored in or introduced into a retrieval system, or transmitted in any form or by any means (electronic, mechanical, photocopying, recording or otherwise), without the prior written permission of the publisher of the book.

Published by Mrs. Veena Arora, for Natraj Publishers, Publications Division, Dehra Dun and printed at Chaman Enterprises, New Delhi.

# ACKNOWLEDGMENTS

In writing this book, I have been helped by my husband, and have extensively used his records and experiences, so that the work is partly his, and I would like to thank him.

I am greatly indebted to my son, Bill, for details of conditions in Borneo and Sarawak, and for nearly all the photographs.

To Lord Hailey, who wrote the Foreword, I am very grateful.

# CONTENTS

vii

Chapter                                           Page

# ILLUSTRATIONS

Elephants bathing . . . *Frontispiece*

# FOREWORD

## by LORD HAILEY

P.C. G.C.S.I. G.C.M.G. G.C.I.E.

(*formerly Governor of the United Provinces, India*)

THERE must be many who still remember the times (now alas! no more) when young men used to debate earnestly the relative advantages and disadvantages of careers in the different Indian services. There was almost always some hesitation about one in particular—the Forest Service. It was obvious that it did fine work and had many attractions, but it also had some drawbacks. There was, for one thing, the prospect of long tours every year in places remote from any chance of other society. It is said that careful mothers used to warn their daughters against marrying into the Forest Service. It might, they said, seem to be very romantic to start with, but it was not so good when you had a family.

If any of these pessimists have read Mrs. Smythies' first book, *Jungle Lady*, they must have felt that in some cases at least their rather gloomy prognostications were very wide of the mark. It is true that for all the earlier years of her Indian life Mrs. Smythies' lines were cast in unusually pleasant places. The headquarters at Naini Tal, that pearl of Himalayan hill stations, with a lake set like a jewel among its seven hills. The bungalow on the terraced slopes of the highest of them, Cheena, within sight of the snowline

xi

of Nanda Devi and Trisul. To the north and east and west
the forested hillsides of Almora and Garhwal; below, the
foothills of the south, the jungles and grassy savannahs of
the Terai and Bhabar, home of every kind of winged and
four-footed game.

All that is true, but there still remained for Mrs. Smythies
the prospect of long months of touring with her husband
in lonely places. Every dictionary of quotations can provide
a mass of axioms from poets and philosophers on the subject of solitude, but none of them seemed to hold a very
direct message for the bride of the Assistant Conservator
of Forests, in Kumaun, fresh from her home in Somerset.
Yet in spite of this lack of guidance from poets and philosophers, Mrs. Smythies does not seem to have been greatly
disturbed by the months of touring in solitary places. She
taught herself to shoot, and sport became a great resource.
There was the constant joy of what is locally known as
"ghooming," or wandering through the jungle on an
elephant in search of game, or simply enjoying the sights
and sounds of jungle life. She had her successes with
leopard and bear and tiger, and her experiences included one
terrifying adventure with a wounded tiger, an episode
unique in its way, but which to be fully appreciated must be
read in the author's own account of it. She savoured to the
full the joys of mahseer fishing in the streams and rivers of
Kumaun. It is not wise to criticize other men's choice in
rivers. Let others have their fancies, but give me the Ramganga, the Nandaur, the Ladhya or the Baramdeo pool on
the Sarda. And Mrs. Smythies had all these for the asking.

But I must not pursue further these nostalgic reveries.
Mrs. Smythies has told fully of her own Kumaun days in
her *Jungle Lady*, and her picture of them is all the more
engaging, because it is a straightforward story, with no
other embellishments than her own appreciation of the
surroundings in which she lived and of her dealings with the

likeable folk of the hills and jungles. And now she has set down more of her memories in a second book. Part of it tells more of her life in Kumaun and it is equally pleasant reading, but there are other memories also, for in after years her husband's work took him farther afield. There are accounts of famine work in the plains of the United Provinces, following on the great drought of 1918, and of seven years forest work in Nepal after Mr. Smythies had retired from the Indian Forest Service. This has a special interest; for though the frontiers of Nepal march for many hundreds of miles with those of India, the Nepalese have always kept their land closed to visitors. There can be very few Europeans who have had so long an opportunity of seeing for themselves the way of life of this interesting people, most of whom still live in the conditions that must have prevailed in India before the arrival of Europeans. There is an account also of journeys which Mrs. Smythies made to Burma, where her son was in the Burma Forest Service, and afterwards to Borneo and Brunei, where he took up forest service when Burma left the Empire in 1947. Of all these experiences she has an interesting story to tell, and she tells it well.

HAILEY

# GLOSSARY

| | |
|---|---|
| *Ayah* | Indian nurse |
| *Bogun* | Container made of bark |
| *Chaor* | Grassy plain |
| *Characut* | Man who cuts food for elephants |
| *Chikor* | Himalayan partridge |
| *Chital* | Spotted deer |
| *Dacoit* | Armed robber |
| *Ekka* | Country pony-trap |
| *Ghat* | Ford |
| *Ghoom* | To wander about on an elephant |
| *Gond* | Swamp deer |
| *Gudjbar* | Iron prong used by mahawats |
| *Gural* | Himalayan chamois |
| *Hakim* | Soothsayer |
| *Hat jao* | Get out |
| *Jharan* | Duster |
| *Jhil* | Small lake |
| *Katola* | A saddle used on elephants |
| *Langur* | Grey monkey |
| *Loo* | Hot west wind |
| *Machan* | Seat for tying in a tree |
| *Mahawat* | Driver of an elephant |
| *Makna* | Tuskless male elephant |
| *Mantra* | Prayer |
| *Pachwa* | Man who stands on rump of elephant |
| *Pug* | Footmark |
| *Puja* | Prayer |

*Glossary*

| | |
|---|---|
| *Saddhu* | Hindu priest |
| *Sanad* | Government order |
| *Sate* | Malayan dish of grilled meat |
| *Serow* | Goat antelope |
| *Sweeper* | Man of low caste who sweeps the house |

CHAPTER ONE

# The Himalayas

"So and no otherwise hillmen desire their Hills!"
A large part of this book is intimately connected with
the Himalayas, rather naturally perhaps since my husband, Evelyn, and I had our home, and lived and worked,
shot and fished, amongst them for many years. A flood of
books about the Himalayas has been published since the
war, mostly written by high level mountain climbers describing the adventures and achievements of expeditions
attacking this or that Himalayan giant. Their viewpoint is
very different. They give the impression that the only
important parts of the great range are those above 15,000
feet, which have an annoying fringe below that level, to
pass through which absorbs and wastes a great deal of time
and money, and both time and money are limited on such
expeditions.

This is all rather misleading, and gives a somewhat
unbalanced view of what the Himalayas really are. We
never approached 15,000 feet, which from a Forest Officer's
point of view is a zone that is treeless, uninhabited, and in
every way, except for scenic effects, useless and unimportant.
Quite a contrast to the viewpoint of Hunt, Evans, Herzog,
and their brother climbers! On the other hand, during
many years we ranged far and wide between the Assam
frontier on the east and Kashmir on the west, a distance of
1,500 miles, travelling on foot, on ponies, on elephants,
occasionally in cars, sampling that "annoying fringe" at a
thousand points. So, for a start, I will attempt to give

the view of how the Himalayas appear to a Forest Officer.

Bounded on the south—as every schoolboy knows—by the Great Plain of Northern India, the Himalayas proper may be roughly defined as the tract between those two great rivers, the Indus and the Brahmaputra, which, rising close together near the sacred Manasarowar lakes, separate and break through the mountain range at points 1,500 miles apart. In that colossal stretch every imaginable variety of conditions is found, of climate, vegetation, fauna, states of human development, religions . . . everything.

But before discussing these, let us for a moment delve into pre-history. First, how long have the Himalayas been there? Well, geologically speaking, a very short time! For most of geological time, i.e. several hundred million years, the site of the future Himalayas was a sea, an extension in fact of the Mediterranean, and only about 30 or 40 million years ago did the Himalayas begin to emerge.

Why are the Himalayas there at all? Scientists tell us, because an irresistible force (the Indian subcontinent moving northwards) met an immovable object (the Tibet-Siberia Shield) and the Himalayas were squeezed up in consequence. Some squeeze!

Is the squeeze finished? Possibly, but the earthquakes that periodically rock this zone suggest that adjustments to great tensions still continue. But, of course, the forces of erosion are continually at work wearing down the mountains—a thickness of deposits equal to the height of Everest has already been removed, and the process will continue until the Himalayas approximate to the Highlands of Scotland.

Enough of geology; let us turn to something of more immediate interest to the Forest Officer—the vegetation. Here we find every possible variation, depending on rainfall and altitude, from the evergreen rain forest on the Assam frontier with 250 inches of rain per annum to the barren rocky scrub slopes of Pakistan with 10 inches, and from the giant bamboos that grow nearly a foot a day to the high altitude dwarf growth of nearly a foot a century.

We sampled the evergreen forest with a tour in the trans-frontier tracts of Assam, the trees festooned with ferns, moss, and orchids, over a 10,000-foot pass, where, incredible as it may sound, we found innumerable marks of a large herd of wild elephants that had been feeding up there *in the snow*! Our trip was into the Momba country, a small tribe, who were nominally Buddhists and so discouraged from taking any form of life. As their neighbours were the savage Dafflas and Akas, who liked nothing better than a head-hunting raid, with a few slaves and attractive young women thrown in, the unfortunate Mombas were at a distinct handicap. In fact, we were told they were in danger of being exterminated, and I felt very sorry for them. As all these tribes were across the frontier in unadministered territory, the Indian Government could do nothing about it.

We travelled 10,000 miles back and forth in the great *sal* belt of the lower foothills, that stretches 700 miles and more from Bengal to the border of the Punjab. And we journeyed through the pine forests of Kumaon, deodar forests around 7,000 feet, and oak forests around the hill stations of Naini Tal and Ranikhet. We also visited the deodar forests of Kulu and the pine and fir forests of Kashmir. Thus we had considerable experience of the principal forests of the Himalayas, which are so valuable for their timber, commercial products, for checking erosion and floods, for supplying the hill populations with innumerable products essential for their welfare.

And what of the hill populations? Here again we find such an amazing medley of races, tribes, creeds, customs, as can scarcely be equalled elsewhere in the world today; from the aboriginal head-hunting Abors and Dafflas of the east to the Kashmiri pundits of the west (Pundit Nehru is one) and the Pathans of the frontier; from the Bhotes of the Nepal foothills, freed from slavery only a generation ago, to the Sherpas of Namche Bazar, or a little higher still, the Abominable Snowman! Nepal alone is alleged to have between twenty and thirty different *languages*, mutually unintelligible. We have camped near aboriginal villages where no white face had ever been seen, and where we required one interpreter to interpret to another to interpret to the villagers!

Creeds and religions? Muslims in the north-west, Hindus in the centre, Buddhists in the north-east, Animists (worshippers of little jungle gods and spirits) and pagans in the south-east, some Christians dotted about near missionary centres, and probably many more I do not know.

It is surely beyond the skill of any writer to describe Himalayan scenery, so savage, so stupendous, so glorious, so infinitely variable. It is certainly beyond mine. I think the most beautiful time was in the Spring, when the hill forests were gay with red rhododendrons and fragrant with bauhinias, and the snow lay low on the high mountains, making them look higher and more ethereal than ever.

There are many hill stations scattered along the mountains, mostly situated on the outer ranges. Ranikhet is one of the most beautiful of these resorts. In our day it was a cantonment used by British troops in the hot weather, where they could have respite from the scorching heat of the plains. The houses and barracks are built among pine trees on a ridge commanding a glorious view of the snow mountains; Nandi Devi (25,660 ft.) and Trisul (23,406 ft.) being 40-45 miles to the north, and Kamet (25,447 ft.) showing up to the north-west.

Evelyn had charge of the forests in the hills for many miles round Ranikhet, but we have not very pleasant memories of Ranikhet itself, for it was here that Evelyn's sister went down with typhoid. We were 30 miles from the cantonment when she fell ill. Knowing something about typhoid, we looked up the symptoms in our medical book, which confirmed our suspicions.

Evelyn sent a messenger to Ranikhet with a note to the doctor in charge there. As it was in the cold weather, the cantonment was empty, but fortunately the doctor had not left. He rode out the 30 miles bringing an ambulance with him. The ambulance was a bed slung on poles, which was carried by coolies, and in this we took the invalid to our forest bungalow at Chaubattia, 4 miles from Ranikhet.

Our fears proved correct, it *was* typhoid. We telegraphed for nurses, but could not hear of any who could come, so Evelyn and I had to do all the nursing for a week till we managed to get two women.

The doctor was extremely kind; he was, however, new to India, and had not had much experience of typhoid. He brought medical books to show us, and asked what we would advise! As the patient had a temperature of 106°, it was a bit alarming.

The washerman ran away. It was against the caste of the other servants to wash the sheets and linen, so I had to make an effort to do it myself. I set to work with a tin tub, a cake of Sunlight soap, and some water which had been heated in an old kerosene tin over a wood fire. Having no one to help me, I found the sheets most awkward to manage. I wrung them out as best I could and hung them up to dry on the apple trees in the garden.

It was a very anxious time. The bungalow had only three rooms, the patient was in one, the nurses had the other two. We had our meals in the verandah; Evelyn and I slept in a tiny tent. We were at an altitude of 7,000 feet, and it was winter! When the sun went down we went to bed, it was too cold anywhere else.

It was six or seven weeks before the patient recovered.

Evelyn had to go off several times on short tours, leaving me to sleep alone in the wee tent. One night I was awakened by bloodcurdling screams coming from the forest, and I feared someone had been attacked by a bear or leopard. Next morning the servants told me that one of them had been chased by a ghost! The people in the mountains firmly believe in ghosts and malignant spirits.

To add to our troubles I noticed that our butler was looking very ill. I questioned him about his health, hoping to be able to do something for him. He told me that his brother had put a curse on him because of a quarrel about land. I tried to persuade him that it was nonsense, and asked the doctor to examine him. He found nothing wrong, but the butler continued to get worse. We tried everything, even giving money to a Hindu priest asking him to cast out the devil, which the butler said was in his stomach. Finally we sent him to the hospital, where he was kept under observation, but although there seemed to be no cause for his condition, he died. The fear of the curse had had this powerful effect on his subconscious mind.

When Evelyn's sister had recovered, and left us, we continued our interrupted tour. Once we were camping in some fallow rice fields at a height of about 4,000 feet. Behind the tents the hill rose steeply, intersected by a rocky ravine. The weather was cold and sunny, all was well, but in the night a violent storm blew up, the rocky ravine became a raging torrent, and the rice fields, made to hold water, were soon flooded. It then began to snow, and Evelyn was afraid the tent would collapse with the weight of it. We dressed, and sat up all night holding on to the poles of the tent. The servants were flooded out; we sent them off for shelter to the nearest village, several miles away. Next day our tent was standing, but it was flooded, the only dry places being our two beds on which we sat marooned. As it was still sleeting, and the servants had not come, we could not move camp. We had some tinned food, and I managed to boil a kettle and heat some sausages over an oil stove. Fortunately the storm was over next day, and we had everything out to dry in the blazing sun. We moved as soon as we could from the rice fields.

All this damp resulted in Evelyn having a bad attack of lumbago. He set out one morning into the forest, and about an hour afterwards I saw him crawling back on all fours. He was most indignant when I laughed; he looked so ridiculous that I could not help it. The servants procured some bear fat, with which they rubbed him, with remarkable effect.

Shooting in the hills is hard work, but I thought nothing of walking up and down a thousand feet. We often went after *gural*, though I did not like the precipices on which they live. Occasionally I shot a barking deer. They live in thick forest, where they move about in a series of bounds and jumps. Their call sounds just like the bark of a dog. The camp had a feast on the days a barking deer had been shot, for their flesh is tender and of good flavour, though I did not eat it myself, for I never liked to eat anything I had shot.

A rare animal, called a serow, lives in these mountains. It is the largest species of goat antelope in the world. When Evelyn first saw one he sent a Forest Guard to catch it, thinking it was a mule which had strayed into the forest; he had not noticed the small horns. If wounded, they are dangerous to approach, for they are liable to attack with their front legs, which have very sharp hooves. Serow became so scarce that they were protected, and shooting them was forbidden.

There were always leopards about, but they are very cunning and not often seen. One day Evelyn came in from his inspection in the forest with the news that he had heard a leopard calling in a ravine about 3 miles away up the mountain. Having been out all day, he was too tired to accompany me, so I set out alone with our head orderly, Jankru Singh. (Government supplied us with three orderlies, who helped with coolies and general camp arrangements; they were usually keen sportsmen.)

Jankru Singh, a typical hillman of Kumaon, carried my 16-bore gun and a coolie carried the *machan* (seat), which we intended to tie up in a tree, and he also led a goat. Our plan was to go to the ravine where the leopard had been calling, find a suitable tree, and tie the *machan* up in it. I would then climb into the *machan* and camouflage myself with leafy twigs. The goat, which had been kept out of sight so that it could not see me climb into the tree, would then be brought up and tied to a tree or stake, where I could see it plainly. Jankru Singh and the coolie would then go off, calling to the goat to follow. The wretched animal, believing itself abandoned, would bleat frantically, and we hoped that any leopard in the vicinity would be attracted to the spot. This may sound cruel, but I always argued that if the leopard were shot the lives of its future victims would have been saved.

When we reached the ravine we could not find a suitable tree for the *machan*. The trees were all chir pines with long straight boles, and not a branch under 40 feet. There was nothing for it but to sit on the ground screened by a bush. I was nervous of doing this, but not liking to appear timid in the eyes of Jankru Singh, I decided to risk it, hoping we would not be charged by a wounded and infuriated leopard.

Jankru Singh and I seated ourselves on the ground behind a small shrub. I loaded my 16-bore with two lethal bullets. The coolie then brought up the goat, which he tied to a stake about 30 yards away, and a few feet below us. Having done this, he walked away calling to the goat to follow. The goat tugged madly at the rope, trying hard to free itself, all the time keeping up a continuous bleating.

We sat like two stone images, hardly daring to breathe.

After a time the goat quietened down, and, to our dismay, it ceased to bleat at all. Our hopes of seeing the leopard began to fade. Jankru Singh rolled a small pebble down the slope, which started the goat calling again, but it soon stopped. Jankru Singh rolled another pebble, and another. Each time the goat gave a feeble bleat, but it had evidently spotted us, and the game was up.

We were thinking of going home when suddenly, with a bound and a scurry, a large leopard sprang on the goat. I waited till the leopard was standing still over his dead victim, I then took careful aim between his eyes and fired. He fell over, shot through the brain. I was thankful that I had not wounded him, for a wounded leopard in the mountains is a nasty problem; he must be finished off at all costs lest he should take to man-eating, and play havoc in the country for miles around. We tied the leopard to a branch, and Jankru Singh and the coolie staggered home with it in triumph.

One of our camps was near a sacred hill called Kailas. We heard that very fine *gural* were to be found on the cliffs there, also that it was a very good place for *chikor*, a species of partridge, so taking our guns and rifles and accompanied by Jankru Singh we set out one morning before sunrise.

In scrub jungle, bordering some fields, we put up a large covey of *chikor*. We both fired two barrels, and did not touch a feather. I am not very expert with a gun, but Evelyn was a good shot, and he was surprised he had drawn a blank. We followed up the covey, and the same thing happened again. We found more coveys, we fired a number of cartridges, and not one partridge did we hit. Evelyn could not understand how, or why, his shooting had deteriorated in this annoying way. About midday we came on a small temple, tucked away in a ravine, surrounded by banana trees; an old *Saddhu* was standing outside watching us. We hailed him and went up to have a chat. After an exchange of salaams and polite greetings, he told us that it was quite useless for us to try and shoot anything on this holy mountain, where all animals and birds were protected by a goddess; it was merely waste of cartridges, time, and energy. We thanked him, and said we wished we had met him earlier in the day. There was something very odd about that mountain, which Evelyn could not explain.

# CHAPTER TWO

# A Man-eating Tigress

IT IS one of the trials of India that every drop of milk has to be boiled, also every drop of drinking water. The servants cannot be trusted to do this; they are quite capable of just heating the milk and afterwards adding some cold unboiled water to dilute it. Being almost immune to typhoid themselves, they cannot understand the necessity for sterilizing milk and water. Having had one experience of typhoid, which had been caused by contaminated milk in one small cup of tea, I determined to take every precaution myself. In some districts, where the water was especially suspect, we distilled it in a small portable still, which was very efficient.

One morning Evelyn was out early. Looking down from a hill near the camp, he saw the cowman prepare to milk the cow. Evelyn had a pair of field-glasses with him through which he watched the proceedings. I had given the cowman a cake of soap, and a towel, with instructions that he must always wash his hands, and the cow's udders, before milking. The cowman had some water in his pail with which he washed his hands. He then milked the cow into the pail without throwing away the dirty water! After that, I always supervised the milking of the cow. Anyway, we might consider ourselves lucky that it was possible to obtain milk. In this respect we were better off than a friend of Evelyn's, who had been posted to Burma. On his first tour he had ordered his servants to bring him some milk. They informed him that none was obtainable. He refused to believe this, and insisted that some should be brought. After a long time his servants produced a large cupful, saying that there were only two nursing matrons in the village, and they could not supply any more! In Burma cows are not milked, they are only kept for the production of bullocks.

Our servants did not like camping in the mountains, especially in the winter months, and I could not blame them. It was terribly cold, and often there was a shortage of food. We found it impossible to keep a good cook, and we had a succession of very indifferent ones. We dismissed one man, who was too bad even for us, and put on a friend of the butler. He had been with us about two weeks when one morning in our postbag, which was brought out from head-quarters by our own postman, was an anonymous letter informing us that our new cook was a leper!

We were, of course, greatly perturbed. We sent the cook off post-haste to the nearest doctor, and anxiously awaited his verdict. I was so alarmed that, when the doctor said the man had no symptoms of leprosy, I wanted a second opinion before I allowed him to work for us again. The anonymous letter must have been sent by the cook we had dismissed. There were many lepers in the hills; we often saw them begging by the wayside, and a terrible sight they were.

Evelyn's work took him into a very remote part of the Division, where we heard that there was a man-eating tigress with cubs. We hoped we might have a chance of shooting this pest, which was terrorizing the countryside. In those days village men had no guns, therefore no defence against such dangers. We knew that a report would be brought to us if the tigress made a new kill.

There were no bungalows in this part of the Division, so we were obliged to live in tents. We had two small ones for ourselves; one we used as a bedroom, the other as a general living room. Knowing that there was a man-eating tigress in the neighbourhood, I did not feel very safe. At night I ran from one tent to the other with my heart in my mouth, imagining that the tigress was waiting to pounce on me out of the darkness.

One day some villagers came with the news that the tigress had killed an old woman who had gone out from her home to cut grass. They asked us to accompany them to the village and then follow up the tigress. If we found any human remains, Evelyn decided we would sit up over them, as there might be a chance the brute would return to finish what was left of her grisly meal.

The village was about 5 miles away, and to get there we walked through some magnificent fir forest. The trees towered 120 feet into the sky, the scent of them was over-powering, and the ground was carpeted with their pungent needles.

The villagers guided us to the spot where the old woman had been seized. The grass she had cut lay scattered on the ground; we found her sickle and some rags of clothing, also large splashes of blood. We scrutinized the ground very carefully and were able to follow a faint blood trail. Evelyn and I had our rifles ready, while the villagers and our orderlies followed the blood marks. We advanced very slowly for about 100 yards. It is nervous work when one is expecting a tigress to spring on one at any moment, the chances being that she will attack before she has been spotted.

We found several bits of clothing, and then we came on the unfortunate woman's head. A small boy, who was following us, ran forward, picked up the head, and said, "Yes, it is my Grannie." A little farther on we found more remains, which were a most gruesome sight; the legs and most of the body had been eaten, only the arms remained.

We had brought a large *machan* with us, which the order-lies tied up in a tree; Evelyn and I climbed into it. The villagers then went off shouting and yelling, hoping that the tigress would hear, and think it would be safe for her to come back and finish what was left of her victim.

We sat very still, praying that the tigress would return before it was too dark for us to see to shoot. Far away on the mountain above us we heard a *sambar* give his hoarse bell of alarm. Our hearts beat faster, for the *sambar*'s call told us that the tigress was on the move. Again he belled, and then again. Would the tigress come into our view? I prayed she would, but I feared she was too clever. Evelyn had told me that man-eaters are always very cunning when they have made a human kill, for their instinct seems to warn them that they have committed an unforgivable crime.

Our hopes sank with the sun. When it was too dark to see we climbed out of the tree. We lit a lantern, which we had brought with us, and made our way back to the village. I did not enjoy that walk for I imagined tigers ready to spring behind every bush, and I was thankful when we reached the bright fires of the village.

The villagers told us that the tigress hunted over a large tract of country, killing someone in one village, and then going off many miles to pounce on a fresh victim. Women were usually taken as they go into the forest to cut grass where it is easy for a tiger to stalk them. The tigress, they said, had two cubs, and she was teaching them to follow her evil ways. They told us a dreadful story about two men of their community.

These two men had gone out to cut grass. Suddenly the tigress had jumped on one of them, the other managed to climb a tree to safety. This unfortunate soul had to watch the agonies of his friend. Two cubs joined their mother, who let go of the man. The poor wretch crawled away towards the tree, where his frantic friend was waiting to give him a hand, imploring him to make haste. He had almost reached the tree and safety when one of the cubs jumped on him and began to maul him. The tigress then drove off the cub, and once more the man crawled away, but only to be jumped on again. This happened several times, the tigress and cubs played with him as a cat does with a mouse, while his friend looked on in a frenzy of despair.

The men were not missed from the village till next day, and it was two days before the survivor was rescued in a state of collapse.

We walked home by the light of a lantern, making as much noise as we could. It was eerie walking through the silent forest. At any other time I would have enjoyed the distant view of the snow mountains in the moonlight, but tonight my one thought was to get back to our camp and safety.

Now that we knew that the tigress was near the camp, Evelyn thought that we should take some precautions. Our post-runner was afraid to travel alone, so another man had to be engaged to accompany him. As they had no weapons I think they were very brave to go along the roads at all.

We tied up buffalo baits, but these were scorned by the tigress. Evelyn had his work to do, so could not give his entire time to hunting the brute.

One morning Evelyn saw the fresh footmarks of the tigress and two cubs on a bridle path close to our camp. He hastened back to warn everyone not to leave the camp except in a large party. He then divided all available men into watches of three men, who were to guard the camp day and night. We mustered a dozen, not counting Evelyn and myself. We had two rifles and two shotguns. We collected dry branches and twigs from nearby, not daring to go far into the forest, and with these we made a bonfire when it was dark. We also lighted three lanterns, placing them on poles round the tents.

It was a fine night and there was frost. We knew the tigress was near because a barking deer gave his alarm call about 10 p.m., and shortly after some *langurs* (grey monkeys) set up a loud chatter not far from the tents. Several times I fancied I saw the glint of eyes under the trees. It was terrifying to feel that we were almost certainly being watched, and possibly stalked, by this terrible man-eater.

When the *langurs* began to call, Evelyn roused everyone in the camp. We all shouted and banged tins, we also added branches to the bonfire. Every now and then Evelyn fired a shot in the air; I kept my gun in my hand. About midnight we were startled to extra vigilance by a loud reverberating and furious roar, followed by a rumbling growl. My blood ran cold as I clutched my gun, shivering with fright. The roars were repeated several times during the night, and each time we all shouted and brightened the fires. There was no doubt at all it was the man-eating tigress that was circling our camp.

Had we been in a bungalow I would not have been nervous, but only having tents for protection, it was very unpleasant. We none of us had any sleep. The tigress was near most of the night, and her departure at dawn was signalled by some *langurs* calling in the distance, and a *sambar* belled on a hill beyond. We were enormously relieved to know that she had gone. We would have given much to be able to follow her till we had a chance of shooting her, but Evelyn had urgent work elsewhere, so reluctantly we marched away. Later that great slayer of man-eaters, Jim Corbett, hunted her down and shot her.

We had a bungalow in Naini Tal, where we lived during the Rains. When we were on tour it was shut up and left in the care of our gardener. That year the ayah had asked me to lock away her silver ornaments in one of the cupboards, but not considering it a safe place, I had sent them with our silver to the bank. It must have become known that the ayah had thought of leaving her valuables in the bungalow. Indian servants usually invest any spare money in silver ornaments, which they sell again by weight when times are hard; they much prefer this method of keeping money to putting it in a bank.

One day we had a postcard from our gardener, and a notice from the police, informing us that our bungalow had been broken into. As they did not know the contents of the various rooms and cupboards, they requested us to come at once.

As soon as Evelyn's work would allow him, we went in that direction. He was very worried about his stamp collection, which he had left in a tin box (soldered down) in one of the cupboards. Our bedroom was in an indescribable mess. The thieves had evidently been searching for the ayah's jewellery. They had ripped open an eiderdown quilt, feathers were everywhere. Many of my clothes were missing, but there on the floor was the tin box containing Evelyn's precious stamps! The thieves had lit a fire with which they had heated a poker, in an attempt to melt the solder, but something had evidently disturbed them, for they had left the box unopened. Nothing mattered as long as the stamps were safe. Had the thieves succeeded in opening the box they might not have taken the stamps, but they might easily have ruined them by throwing them into the garden, which at that time of year was deep in snow.

Naini Tal is bitterly cold in the winter; I do not think I have been so cold anywhere else. Our bungalow, built on a ridge, was 7,000 feet above sea level. None of the doors or windows fitted properly, icy blasts blew through cracks and crevices, and the chimneys all smoked. Above the rooms a loft, in which innumerable rats lived and thrived, ran the length of the house. We could hear them scampering to and fro, rolling things around (possibly walnuts), and sometimes making such a din with their chorus of squeaks that we were kept awake. We put down traps and poison, but never succeeded in exterminating the rats. Occasionally they would

c

come into the rooms, and I once had one on my bed. I gave such a scream that Evelyn nearly died of heart failure!

Perhaps worse than the rats were the scorpions. In the monsoon it was never safe to go without shoes. We found scorpions on the floor, in our shoes, in our beds and in our sponges. On one occasion when Evelyn rubbed his face with a sponge, he felt something hard, which turned out to be a scorpion! There were also snakes. One evening Evelyn opened a door in the dark and felt a sharp stab on his thumb. He hastily switched on the light, and there, on the latch of the door, was a small snake! He called to me, and, when I heard what had happened, I felt frozen with horror. I rushed for the snake-bite outfit, while Evelyn killed the snake, which he examined closely. From the marks on its head he decided it was of a non-poisonous species, and he refused to do more than lance the place and apply permanganate crystals. I was not at all sure we ought not to amputate his thumb then and there, but he scorned any such drastic treatment, and went off to bed and to sleep. I watched him anxiously for several hours till I knew there was no danger. It is as well to study, and be able to recognize, the different kinds of snakes. The servant of one of our friends was bitten on the big toe by a snake in the jungle far from any medical aid. Our friend seized an axe and, without any hesitation, chopped off the man's toe. The snake was killed and sent for identification. It was a harmless grass snake!

# CHAPTER THREE

# Duck Shooting

BIRD shooting in the mountains is not easy, and *chikor* shooting is exceedingly difficult, besides being very strenuous. When the covey rose I always seemed to be climbing over a wall, or in the wrong place. I found this exasperating when I had toiled up several hundred feet for a shot.

Pheasant shooting is also difficult in the hills. One has to take a snap at a bird as it flashes across a narrow opening in the trees. I was much too slow, the bird had gone almost before I had seen it. We had a couple of spaniels, which were excellent gun dogs. They were trained and looked after by our old sweeper.

There was always the danger of leopards, which are very partial to dog flesh. Even in Naini Tal they lurk on the hill-sides, ready to pounce on pet dogs being taken for a walk. We had a leopard living in the grounds of our bungalow. I saw him occasionally at dusk; at night time he would walk boldly past the verandah and go down the path to the gate. We knew when he was about from the alarm calls of porcupines, which were such a nuisance in the garden, digging up all our pet bulbs and roots.

To protect our dogs when we were shooting we gave them collars studded with spikes an inch long. A leopard usually kills a dog by seizing its neck. Our dog Peter was attacked on three different occasions by leopards, and each time he escaped unharmed, saved by his spiky collar.

A hungry leopard is very daring. Once a leopard jumped

on Peter when he was only a few yards ahead of Evelyn on a path. All Evelyn had was a heavy stick, but he attacked the leopard with it, and in the excitement of the moment he even kicked the leopard which, fortunately, slunk away and did not attack Evelyn as it so easily might have done.

I had never done any duck or snipe shooting as they do not occur in the hill forests, so I was very excited when I was invited by a senior official to a duck shoot on a *jhil* in the plains. Evelyn had to go to Calcutta on business connected with his turpentine and rosin factory, so could not accompany me.

Knowing so little about duck shooting, I was nervous that I should probably make a fool of myself. I tried to read up something about it, but could find nothing very helpful. My lack of knowledge was only exceeded by my abundance of enthusiasm. I spent most of the night before the shoot dreaming of birds, solitary and otherwise, coming over high and fast, and myself, to wit, bringing them down with pretty shots in numbers to fill a cart.

We started off on a peerless Indian cold weather morning (before sunrise, as we had some way to go), with a glorious nip in the air, and the piercing smoke of dung-cake fires in our nostrils, and wreaths of morning mist hanging low over the palms and the tamarinds, while the dome of sky graded from saffron to gold. Absorbed at first in the appeal of the scene and the fascination of new things, I forgot the object of our excursion, and then, suddenly remembering my ignorance of *jhils*, and the shooting of *jhils*, I started a stream of questions to quench my thirst for knowledge.

Presently we arrived at a beautiful little lake surrounded by swamp grasses, with two convenient little islands of reed well out near the middle.

"Don't shoot at shoveller," Mr Cox remarked, as we waded out and separated, and I was left to ponder what a "shoveller" might be.

The beaters began at one end of the *jhil*, and when one of them fired off his muzzle-loader with the report of a cannon, a myriad of birds of all sorts and shapes and sizes and colours rose circling over the water. Two or three sorts of crane, various flocks of paddy birds, geese, at least four sizes and species of duck, and oddments of water-loving birds past all counting, came honking and swishing and flitting over-head and around, and I had struck the first difficulty of what to shoot and what to leave alone.

The jungly *shikari*, who had been sent with me to pick up my birds (and an idle man he was that day), seemed to know no better than I, and anyhow he did not understand my Hindustani.

"*Achcha shikar?* (Good shooting?)" I said with a queried intonation, pointing at some large white birds rapidly approaching, and he grunted something unintelligible. Their long curved yellow bills did not look ducky, so I let them go.

Then a large black-and-white bird with a duck's flight rushed past, and I let drive both barrels with no result. Next a V-shaped flight of smaller birds (teal I imagined, and was not wrong) raced over with a soughing of wings, but never a feather quivered to my shots.

And so for the next ten minutes the fun was furious until my barrels were hot, and I was hot, surrounded by a ring of empty cases, and the *shikari* stood behind me patiently waiting to go and retrieve something.

Towards the end, even to my untrained eyes, the birds seemed a powerful long way up, and as Mr Cox's fusillade had stopped, I stopped too. But suddenly a solitary fool of a duck soared down and settled on the water just in front of my island, and in easy range.

Reader, have you never experienced the temptation of the sportsman who, having blazed and blazed with nothing to show for it, suddenly sees the chance of secretly retrieving

his reputation, and producing something for the bag with a
sitting shot?

I was tempted and fell. Dashing out into the water to
recover him before he disappeared, I saw he was a very
lovely duck (and my first), with a ruddy brown breast, fawn
coloured neck, and black-and-white wings. I bore him
triumphantly across to Mr Cox.

"Well, what luck!" he sang out, and I held up my bird
with pride.

"Mm, a Brahminy," he remarked disparagingly.

Disconcerted by the tone rather than the words, I made
the best of it. "Yes, a very fine plump one," I replied.

"Maybe," said Mr Cox, "but they are not shot." Now
how was I to know that? "And look here, dear lady," he
went on, "I said thirty *yards* not *miles*. Some of those birds
you were wasting cartridges on at the end could not have
heard your gun, much less felt it."

Depressed and sad, I apologized for my unfortunate con-
tribution to the bag, the while I examined Mr Cox's, which
included several mallard, teal and pintail.

"We will give this place a rest and try for some snipe
farther on," suggested Mr Cox, and we moved off. "You
will want eights now," he added.

A sudden thought struck me, and I looked into my
bag.

"I have not many eights left," I said ruefully, "I have
been drawing from the wrong bag by mistake."

"Well you can't expect much of a bag if you shoot at high
flying geese and duck with number eight shot; contrariwise,
as Tweedledee would say," said Mr Cox laughing. Anyhow, I felt I was learning how and what not to shoot, which
is the first step to knowledge.

We went off to some swampy reeds and cut rice fields a
mile away, and almost at once a bird whirred up with a twit,
but was out of sight before I was nearly ready to fire.

"Don't stand and gaze at them," sang out Mr Cox. "You have to shoot quickly at snipe."

The next bird that got up I did shoot quickly, very quickly, like the advertisement of smokeless diamond. I shot "quick as lightning," and to my joy the bird dropped. To be quite accurate it dropped separately and widely, in small bits, a beak here and a toe there and a tail feather somewhere else, as the full charge hit it at about five yards' range.

"Never mind," said Mr Cox highly amused, "it was only a snippet."

"The word denotes a small snipe, but the complete sentence suggests another sort of Brahminy?" I queried.

"That's about it," said Mr Cox, chuckling to himself. He was shooting like a book, and thoroughly happy with himself, so my little and varied contretemps acted as a piquant sauce to his humour.

Presently, after wasting a few more cartridges on the morning air, I suddenly began to tumble to the knack of shooting at a snipe without conscious aim, and when, after a bit, two birds rose together, which jinked rather less than usual, I succeeded in dropping both, I could scarce forbear to cheer, and even Mr Cox made an encouraging remark.

After a peaceful and well-watered interval (snipe shooting under an Indian sun is thirsty work) I suggested tentatively that I was burning to retrieve the Brahminy episode, so with half an hour still to fit in before returning, we again visited the *jhil*.

As we waded out and exchanged stations, we could see that a fair number of birds had settled down again. The proceedings, outwardly, were much as before, but in myself I felt much happier. Everyone on his first visit to a *jhil* must inevitably feel confused and bewildered at the wild medley of birds that come over, and hesitation and doubt what to shoot at, and what to leave alone, produce that uneasiness of mind with which good shooting is impossible.

Favoured by two or three low-flying stragglers, I succeeded in bagging a few, while Mr Cox added several more to the bag. It had been a wonderful day for me.

PLATE I    "The head of a great pool on the Ramganga, where the monsters of the river lurk in the depths."

# CHAPTER FOUR

# *A Paradise on Earth*

AFTER we had spent several years in the mountains, Evelyn was transferred to a Division in the foothills. Our touring now was so much easier, for we rode on elephants instead of walking up and down steep forest paths, and the climate was perfect in the cold weather. Not so healthy, of course, and extremely hot in the months before the rains, but then I went up to our bungalow in Naini Tal. I did not want to run the risk of getting malaria, and I am thankful to say I never had an attack of it. As I have lived in some of the most malarious jungles of the world I consider I was fortunate, and my escape was, I think, due to the elaborate precautions I always took to guard against mosquitoes. In those days the only prophylactic we had was quinine.

When Evelyn took over his new Division he found himself saddled with a peculiar legacy from his predecessor, an officer of highly ingenious, if somewhat unpractical, ideas. He had been asked to procure a *live* tiger for a Zoo. He had constructed an enormous sort of mousetrap, about 10 feet long and 6 feet high, with iron bars as thick as a man's finger along the sides and one end. The trap was divided into two partitions, a small portion to hold the bait—a young buffalo in lieu of cheese—and a large partition to hold the tiger. The open end of the main partition had an iron-sheet door, held up by a hook attached by wire to a trigger in the smaller partition, which the tiger would probably release when he tried to get at the young buffalo, and cause the iron-sheet to fall with a loud clang. The whole trap was then placed on a wooden platform, which had four solid wooden wheels below, and a shaft in front to which a pair of bullocks could be yoked. There was a wooden ramp behind, up which a tiger could conveniently walk into the trap.

This wonderful Heath-Robinson contraption having been prepared, it was then dragged by bullocks to a spot about a dozen miles from Ramnagar station to the top of a 2,000-foot pass. The road up to—or down from—this pass had a number of hairpin bends (quite like the final test of the Monte Carlo rally!), and was difficult at the best of times for bullock carts to negotiate.

How anyone could imagine that two unfortunate and terrified bullocks were going to drag the trap, complete with dead young buffalo and infuriated raging tiger, down that twisting road passed our comprehension when we heard about it. And that was quite soon! For the incredible fact was that this Heath-Robinson outfit actually did trap a tiger!

Evelyn knew nothing about it as his predecessor, when giving over charge, had forgotten to mention the legacy of producing a live tiger for a Zoo. So Evelyn was astounded to get an urgent message one morning from a worried Forest Ranger that a tiger had been caught, and he did not know what to do as the bullocks refused to be harnessed to the cage.

We hastily jumped on an elephant and went off at her best pace, about 5 miles an hour, to the pass, where in the depths of *sal* forest we had our first view of the great mousetrap. It was quite a sight. The poor little buffalo was dead, scragged to pieces by the tiger's claws, and the tiger was just crazy, roaring madly, and striking the iron door and iron bars with his paws. It was not surprising that the bullocks refused to be harnessed to the trap.

I do not know how professional animal catchers cope with such a situation, and Evelyn's forestry training at Oxford did not cover such problems. It was quite obvious, however, that bullocks were not the correct answer. Evelyn told the Ranger to send to Ramnagar for some large iron hooks (to hook fore and aft) with long strong ropes attached, and to recruit twenty or thirty men to hold on to the ropes, and thus pull or brake the carriage down to Ramnagar. As all this would take time, it was decided to have everything ready early the next morning, when the attempt would be made. There was a small forest bungalow nearby, called Sultan, where we retired to spend the night, and left the tiger to quieten down before morning.

At daybreak next day a large party, consisting of ourselves, the Ranger and Forest staff, and a gang of volunteers for handling the ropes, set off to the trap. To our astonishment we found it empty! During the night the tiger had managed to force two iron bars apart sufficiently wide to squeeze through, and had escaped. This gives an idea of a tiger's strength. Personally I was quite glad the tiger was free again, and not condemned to spend the rest of his life in a zoo.

Evelyn's new Division was in glorious country, which abounded with game of every description, and through which ran two splendid rivers; not mighty ones as Himalayan rivers go, but smaller ones, which rose in the lower mountains.

It was in these rivers that I first learned to fish. Bright sunny days without a cloud were the best for fishing; even a few tiny clouds seemed to put the fish down. I wore a pair of pleated shorts, and waded up to my knees. The water was not cold; I could paddle for hours without catching a chill. The stones under the water were very slippery, and I often fell in and got soaking wet. For mahseer we usually fished with different sized spoons, made by

our orderlies from old cigarette tins. We also used dead
bait for larger fish. We went out from 10 a.m. to 3 p.m.;
before, or after, it was not much use.

The Ramganga was our favourite river. If, when I die, I
am told at the Pearly Gates that my soul may not immediately enter Paradise, but that I may choose anywhere
on earth to dwell, until the time is ripe, I shall have no
difficulty in making my choice. My soul would be at peace
in the valley through which flows this lovely river. It is an
earthly paradise to which my inadequate pen fails to do
justice.

The wild unruly Ramganga runs throughout its whole
length untrammelled by the works of man; the Canal
Department knows it not. To the lover of the remote places
of the earth, of untrodden paths, and the silent illimitable
spaces, it makes an appeal altogether irresistible. Changing
with the changing seasons, the river and its surroundings
remain ever unchanged in this characteristic of wildness and
solitude. Not the blank solitude of deserts or the polar
regions, but rather that perfect solitude teaming with all
manner of life except man, and to be found only in inaccessible backwaters far from the haunts of civilization.

The river debouches from the foothills of the Himalayas
into the flat Bhabar country in a wide stony bed, surrounded
on either side by thick scrub forest and broad bands of
heavy grass, the home of uncounted deer and carnivora.

A small bungalow, and two or three grass huts installing
peripatetic shopkeepers, represent the last outpost of
civilization and of shops. Thence for 8 miles upstream the
river has broken its way through the last rampart of mountains in a precipitous and lonely gorge, where great slabs of
bare yellow sandstone and vertical rock strata alternate with
deep-sided ravines dripping with moisture, and covered
with maidenhair ferns, and all manner of tropical creepers
and orchids clinging to the dark evergreen forest trees.

Through this gorge flows the river, now with its voice hushed in a long, deep, mysterious pool, now foaming over boulders in a roaring cataract where the big mahseer lie to feed, or again swirling with a subdued mutter past occasional sandbanks, or half submerged rocks, where crocodiles love to bask; and everywhere the footmarks of *sambar* and of the little barking deer, of tiger and leopard and wild dog, which lie in wait to catch and kill their prey by the roar of the great waters.

Everywhere also the wonderful translucent blue-green colour of the river, reflecting both the vivid blue of the sky and the equally vivid green of the tropical foliage of the gorge. At the top of the gorge a tributary stream comes in, the "River of Gold," where, from the upper sandy reaches, occasional small parties of gold-washers obtain a bare 8 annas worth of gold for each long working day.

But of greater interest to the fisherman is the junction of this stream with the main river, a roaring, foaming rapid swirling around great boulders at the head of a great pool, where the monsters of the river lurk in the depths and go up to the junction to feed.

Here, once, Evelyn got into a fish which went with its first headlong rush into the pool and stayed there, and nothing would move it. All the strain that a strong man could exert with a powerful 16-foot salmon rod and un-breakable wire trace had no effect on it for several hours, nor half a ton of boulders thrown in to move it, nor even the appearance of an elephant, which was pushed in three times to try and dislodge it.

Finally a local hunter, who could dive and swim like an otter, was urged to dive down and stir the fish up, but he firmly refused to go into the pool at all, being convinced that, in some mysterious way, a crocodile had been hooked and was at the other end of the line. So Evelyn, with throbbing arms, and a backache that lasted a week, reeled in his line as short as possible, straightened his rod, and taking off the reel, put a loop of the line round the tail of the elephant, which was then urged to walk away! Unfortunately, but not unexpectedly, the line broke, and the size of the monster that was hooked remained for ever in doubt. It was probably a *goonch*, a fresh-water shark with an immense flat head, which it pushes underneath a rock when hooked, and remains immovable. A friend of ours was once playing a 40-lb. mahseer when an enormous *goonch* attacked it, and on landing the mahseer he found that a large piece had been bitten out of it. The next day, fishing in the same place, he hooked and landed, after several hours, a 150-lb. *goonch*, which was probably the attacker of the previous day. The two whiskers on each side of its mouth were as large as the handle of a tennis racquet.

Above this junction the character of the river alters, and the most perfect part of this most perfect river commences. Imagine a broad, flat valley of old river terraces, 2 to 3 miles broad and 15 miles long, covered for the most part with great seas of waving tiger grass, with occasional islands of *sal* and scattered trees of *dhak* and *semal*, and along the river itself dense thickets and islands of *shisham*. To the south a low scarp of hills, sloping down into the grassy savannah in broad, gently sloping sheets of dense *sal* forest; to the north a higher ridge of hills, rising 2,000 feet above the river level, clothed from top to bottom with luxuriant tropical forest, and broken up into a wild medley of little side ravines and ridges. Meandering down the valley, sometimes on one side and sometimes on the other, flows the river between broad beds of boulders and sand, and bordered by tufty grasses and *shisham* thickets. No longer do we find the unfathomable pools and wild grandeur of the gorge, but the river flows crystal clear, quiet and sparkling, over broad stretches of gravel, ending in a short stretch of rapids running into a pool, which again tails off into a broad reach of gently flowing water. No longer do we find the monsters of the gorge, but the water swarms with their smaller brothers running from 1 to 8 or occasionally 10 pounds.

But the crowning glory of this most glorious valley is its absolute wildness, where elephants wander freely and the tiger roams at will. Hidden away in the depths of leagues of primeval forest, an occasional forest hut or a still more occasional rest house are the only signs of human habitation; not a village or hamlet in all this stretch spoils its virgin wildness. Here, as nowhere else, nature is unspoilt by contact with man, and the methods and manners of the beasts of the forest can be studied intimately and at first hand. When the grass plains are burnt, and the young grass comes up, the eaters of grass—the *chital* (spotted deer), hog deer and barking deer—come out in the dusk to graze, from the shady *sal* forests and *shisham* thickets, where they have laid up for the day.

Naturally the eaters of flesh, which prey on the concentrated herds, are concentrated also. The hours of darkness, and more especially the hours of dusk, soon after sunset, ring to the melodious danger call of the *chital*, the harsh bell of the *sambar*, or the persistent bark of a barking deer which has spotted the slinking form of a leopard, or perhaps a tiger stalking down boldly for a drink. More rarely (but yet not so very rarely if one is lucky) the feline is met with hunting his meat from God, and once in the gloaming we stood absorbed and unobserved, watching a tiger stalk a herd of *chital* to a successful conclusion.

This also is the breeding season of the *chital*, and the hoarse screaming challenge of the stags adds a note of indescribable appeal to the voices of the forest. Moving quietly along the edge of the forest, it is no uncommon sight to see two stags with clashing antlers and striving quarters fighting for the possession of the herd.

Gradually the valley closes in, and again the river is running in a narrow precipitous gorge, even grander and more inspiring than the lower one, with tier upon tier of dense forest slopes rising up steeply 1,000 feet above the river level. Here again the river flows with great foaming rapids running into deep, cavernous, overhung pools. As the gorge is ascended it becomes wilder and wilder, until the last 2 or 3 miles become almost impossible to penetrate. Here also the whole bank of the river is marked with the tracks of *sambar* and the footprints of tiger, but seldom is a human footprint to be seen. Then abruptly the dense forest ends and the valley passes into bare precipitous mountains dotted with hill villages and terraced cultivation, the river is no longer a jungle river, and the great charm of its unspoilt wildness ends.

For over 30 miles the river and its valley afford such a tract of glorious country to the sportsman and naturalist, to the artist and lover of wild nature, that, once known, it can draw one back to the infinite charm of so perfect an environment.

While the cold weather in the submontane forests is simply glorious from the point of view of climate, scenery, and health, the early hot weather also has infinite attractions. Every three years or so we witnessed the miracle of a big *sal* seed year. Have you seen the massed blossom in the fruit orchards of England in the Spring? Replace the pink blossom on 15- or 20-foot-high apple trees by cream blossom on 100-foot-high *sal* trees, and expand it to 1,000 square miles, and you will have a faint idea of what a *sal* flowering is like. From the tops of the hills it is a wonderful sight to see the sombre green of the *sal* belt gradually turn to creamy white, stretching as far as the eye can see.

Touring in these forests at this time, we can see and appreciate at close range the riot of colour of the flowering trees, the creamy blossom of the *sal* forming a general background to the purple *Bauhinias*, the mauve *sandan*, the red *semal*, the golden flame-of-the-forest, and many other species. In the evening, sitting out in the open in our camp chairs, we would hear perpetually the tonk-tonk of night-jars, the monotony of the coppersmith, the screech of parrakeets going to roost, the soft calls of little owls. Mingled with these bird noises would be the ringing challenge of *chital* stags claiming mastery of the herd, the occasional sawing call of a leopard, or the reverberating boom of a wandering tiger. And when night had fallen, it was a joy to get into our camp beds under the sky, with the scent of the blossom in our nostrils, the sounds of the jungle in our ears, and the stars twinkling through our mosquito curtains in our sleepy eyes.

D

# CHAPTER FIVE

## *In Tiger-land*

IN CAMP there is so little else to do that I think one is apt to become too absorbed and enthusiastic about *shikar*. Some people develop a phobia about it, and grow so selfish that they are jealous of others shooting at all. When Evelyn was very junior, he was actually forbidden to shoot tigers and leopards as a very senior officer wanted all the shooting for himself and his parties.

Had we been so inclined, we could have shot a great many tigers in the many years we camped in the jungles. It is, however, the first one or two tigers that fall to one's rifle that provide the greatest thrills, and after that we did not make any special efforts to shoot tigers, but merely hunted any that were cattle killers.

The forest is divided into blocks for shooting, which are open for two weeks each month, and can be booked by sportsmen on payment of a small sum. For the remaining two weeks the blocks have a rest period, only Forest Officers and District Officers may shoot. Evelyn, of course, had a tour programme, and could book ahead the blocks through which we would be passing; he tried so to arrange matters that we could shoot wherever we happened to be. Forest Officers had another advantage, and a very useful one, for they always had with them one or two Government elephants, without which shooting is very much more difficult. We were lucky to have a wonderful *mahawat* called Bisharat Ali, a Mahommedan of course, clean shaven with sharp aquiline features. He was a keen sportsman,

50

brave as a lion, and very good with his elephant. I was never nervous when he was in control, seated on the elephant's head in front of me.

Day in and day out for seven months of the year we rode elephants. On march days we covered 10 to 12 miles, on other days we often went as far *ghooming* in the forest looking for game. At the end of Evelyn's service we reckoned that we had ridden at least 10,000 miles on elephants. At first their jolting gait gave me a backache, but I gradually became accustomed to it. Sometimes on the march I knitted as we went along, or I learned the names of all the different trees. When I mounted, the elephant was made to kneel and an orderly held the elephant's tail horizontally, making a sort of step. I then pulled myself up by the ropes which harnessed the pad to the back of the elephant. When I wanted to dismount I usually jumped down, and I felt as if I had suddenly become a dwarf, which was a weird sensation.

From an elephant's back, seated on a pad or *katola* (a small bed put upside down on the elephant's back, with the legs sticking upwards), one can see over and into tall grass and bushes, whereas on foot one would see nothing at all, and indeed one could hardly push a way through the dense undergrowth. One man would certainly make much more noise and disturbance than two elephants. It is surprising how quietly these mammoths of the jungle can move. There is no sound of footsteps, only the swish of a branch as it is pushed aside, or the rustle of grass.

We were thrilled with our elephants, and fascinated by the string of twenty camels which we had for carrying our luggage. On a march day while we were having our breakfast we would watch the orderlies and camel men loading the camels; they growled and roared in protest. They had to kneel down while they were being loaded, and to keep them from jumping up suddenly a rope was tied round their knees.

Camels are vicious beasts, they can never be petted; many of them have to wear muzzles, for a camel's bite is a serious thing, and their mouths drip with a foul saliva. On days of rain, or after rain, the camp could not move, for camels cannot walk on wet ground without risk of falling. They slide about in a grotesque manner, their long spindly legs slipping in all directions, until one fears the camel will split in half, or break a leg. Often we had a baby camel going along with our string, and several were born in our camps. The camel men habitually drink camel milk; I tried some once, but thought it tasted like camels' smell, and that is frightful.

Elephants and camels have a mutual hate of each other. We had to be very careful to keep them well apart, for if they met they would both stampede. They never seemed to get used to each other, even after they had lived in the same camp for six or seven months. When the camels stampeded, their loads would come flying off, and it was invariably the crockery box, or the box containing lamps. The butler was an expert packer, and seldom was anything broken even though the box was smashed to pieces.

I had evolved an adequate and, I hoped, foolproof method of packing. There was a partitioned box for the crockery, with baize covers for the different pieces, so that no paper was necessary. There was a box for the silver, a box for the linen, a box for the dusters and another for the dirty ones.

Indian servants use quantities of dusters and dishcloths, all known as *jharans*. Every day I gave out one dozen to the various men, and next day they would be returned absolutely filthy. How they got into this state was a mystery, and one shuddered to think of the manifold, and sometimes dreadful, uses to which they were put. Unless the *jharans* were returned and counted every day, they would disappear gradually till none was left.

In the foothills our favourite and most exciting sport was tiger shooting, either from an elephant or a *machan*. When sitting up in a *machan* it is absolutely essential to sit motionless when waiting for a tiger to return to its kill. Turning the leaves of a book would be enough to attract the attention of a tiger, so it is not advisable to read, and one tiny cough would betray one's presence.

It is not at all easy to sit motionless for hours on end. I have endured agonies of discomfort; my legs went to sleep and seemed to swell, I was bitten all over by vicious red ants and dared not knock them off; horrible black midges danced in front of my eyes and plunged into them; mosquitoes bit my face and hands; my back ached, I ached all over; but I dared not move. Evelyn would not put up with all these discomforts, so he seldom sat up over a kill. Apart from the discomfort I enjoyed sitting up. I was always full of hope that the tiger would appear, and meantime I was intensely interested in the jungle life all around me. I have sat so still that birds have perched within a yard of me, quite unaware of my presence in the tree, and *langurs* have come very close, much too close for my liking.

I had an interesting sit-up once in the jungles near the river Ganges. A tiger had killed one of our small buffaloes and dragged it into a narrow ravine. The kill had been left in a sort of bottleneck, where the ravine was very narrow, and the banks on either side were steep. The only possible tree for a *machan* had a steep bank immediately behind it, so that the top of the tree was below the crest of the bank. The *machan* was tied up in this tree, and I sat facing the kill. On my right the ravine climbed abruptly, and behind was the high bank. To my left the ravine opened on to a dry river bed. The tiger was probably lying up at the top of the ravine.

I had been waiting for over two hours and was becoming stiff and aching all over, being not at all comfortably seated, when suddenly I saw the great head of a tiger high up the ravine above me. My heart raced, as it always did when I saw a tiger. It beat so hard and so fast that I almost suffocated, and I feared the tree might shake. The tiger seemed to be looking straight at me, so I sat very still and watched him. I was afraid even to blink for fear he might catch sight of the movement. He moved forward very slowly, looking magnificent.

I might have tried to bring my rifle round, but I thought it would be too risky, so I decided to wait. I imagined that the tiger would be sure to come on to the kill in due course, and if I moved, even ever so slightly, he might see me and bound away. Moving a step forward, then pausing and listening, and then taking another step, the tiger gradually moved out of my sight behind the tree. I always found it an eerie feeling to be quite alone so close to a tiger, even though I thought I was reasonably safe. A jungle tiger is such a superb animal, so powerful, and so terrific if wounded, that I always had the feeling that he could get me if he really tried, and I often had to assure myself that I was out of his reach in a tree.

I waited and waited, expecting every moment to see the tiger appear from underneath my tree, but nothing happened, all was quiet. Time was getting on, the sun was sinking rapidly, and I knew I should not be able to see my sights for much longer. I decided, therefore, to try and turn my head to look behind me. I did this so gradually that the movement was scarcely perceptible. To my astonishment, there, lying full length on the bank directly behind me, was the tiger, not more than 15 feet away, and slightly above me! I could see every hair on his body. I watched him for a few minutes; he had not seen me, and he was quite unaware of any strange presence. I debated what I ought to do. It was thrilling to watch this splendid beast at such close quarters, but it was rapidly becoming dark, and he showed no inclination to get up and move on to the kill. He blinked his eyes and licked his paws, occasionally his mouth opened into a terrific yawn while I watched fascinated. When it was almost too dark to see I started to try and move my rifle round, but I immediately attracted his attention. He jumped up, snarled and spat furiously at me, and then was off before I had time to fire. Perhaps this was fortunate; Bisharat Ali thought that the tiger might have sprung at me into the tree had he been hit.

I tried again for this same tiger when he killed another buffalo not long afterwards. We had to do a march the morning that he killed, so it was not convenient to sit up that day as the bungalow to which we had moved was 6 miles away. Next morning I got up at 4 o'clock when it was still pitch dark, and mounting Bisharat's elephant, I set out expecting to reach the kill at daybreak, hoping perhaps to see the tiger before he lay up for the day.

It was very cold riding on the elephant, and the tall grass was sopping wet with dew, which it showered on us as we thrust our way through it. Several times animals dashed away in front of us, but we could not see them. Near the kill we saw a very large wild-cat, which had probably been stealing a meal from the tiger's buffalo, lying by a small stream. The carcase was not covered up, which was unusual, and might mean that the tiger had abandoned it, but, on the other hand, there were many vultures sitting in the trees all round, and not one of them was on the kill. This was a good sign, and might mean that the tiger was nearby guarding his meat. As I had come so far I decided to sit up.

I was in the *machan* by 8 o'clock and I sat up the entire day. I endured agonies of discomfort most of the time. The vultures remained in the trees, none of them ventured on to the dead buffalo, so I knew the tiger must be very near. Several times I heard him in the grass behind me, and once he sneezed so loudly that I nearly jumped out of my *machan*.

I think he must have seen me getting into the tree. I made the mistake of not wandering round on the elephant while the *machan* was being tied up, which would have driven the tiger off a little way, and he might not then have noticed me climbing into the tree. I left at sunset and did not reach the camp till 9 p.m., after a long and tiring day. My only meals were some tea and toast at 4 a.m., and some sandwiches before I climbed into the *machan*.

One day our elephant man brought in news that he had found a full-grown buffalo, which had obviously been killed by a tiger, or a pair of tigers. We went to the place about 2 p.m. and the orderlies tied up two *machans*, one about 30 yards from the buffalo and the other some little distance behind in the direction from where we expected the tiger to approach. Evelyn took this *machan*, leaving the one nearer the kill for me. Evelyn had a ·450 double barrel high velocity rifle, and I had my ·256 Mannlicher. I climbed up to the *machan* by a rope ladder. I always disliked doing this as it swayed so violently that I was afraid of falling off. Having hidden ourselves with small branches, we began our long vigil, hoping perhaps to see both the male and female tigers, indicated by the marks of their paws on the ground.

For an hour all was quiet except for the chattering of birds; flights of green parrakeets were darting among the trees, and two red-billed blue magpies came to scold over the kill; occasionally one would have a few pecks in a hurried, frightened sort of way.

Presently we heard footsteps and my heart began to pound. I was keyed up to shoot, but instead of the tiger a great boar appeared, followed by his family of sows and piglets. He was not a perfect gentleman, because he chased his family away while he had a good meal himself, pausing every now and then to listen intently. After a time this family moved off, and all was silent in the forest.

The stillness was again broken by the rustling of leaves,

and again my heart thumped and banged. I was sure the tiger was coming this time, but no, it was only a mongoose, a beautiful one of the large variety, with a fine grey coat. He was very nervous, but snatched a few mouthfuls before he too disappeared.

An hour before sunset footsteps were again heard, very slow and soft, with many pauses. I knew this must be the tiger at last. The steps came from behind my tree, so the tiger must have come into Evelyn's view. The soft pad-pad came on and then stopped, and I heard no more. I dared not move for fear of being seen, so I sat as if frozen. I realized the animal must be sitting close behind my tree, and the slightest movement would betray my presence. It is curious that tigers never seem to scent a human being in a tree. Evelyn watched this one for nearly an hour; he did not shoot as he wanted me to have the shot.

The tiger yawned and stretched, washed his face, and behind his ears after the manner of cats. He then began to play with some elephant droppings, rolling them about like croquet balls, and putting them just like a playful kitten.

Evelyn was beginning to fear that it would be too dark to see before the tiger approached the kill, thus giving me a chance of a shot, and in that case he was going to fire himself. However, it was still fairly light when I heard the tiger get up, and then almost immediately I saw him walk into view. I had a sitting shot looking straight down on his head and neck, a fatal spot. The great beast fell where he stood, a fine male measuring 9 feet 8 inches.

We sometimes saw wild dogs in the forest, the size of a collie and red as a fox; they usually hunt in small packs of six to ten—not in hundreds as Kipling described in the "Jungle Books." The method employed by a pack in killing its prey is, from the human point of view, altogether abominable. The dogs are quite tireless, and hunt their prospective kill—a *sambar*, for example—for miles, in the end usually driving it into an open stream bed, where they eat it still alive.

At that time there was a reward of Rs.50 for every dog killed. One day a cowherd brought to our camp a litter of nine dead small wild dog puppies, which had only just been born. He had seen the bitch go to her burrow, and had waited till she had gone off again before collecting the pups. When Evelyn gave him Rs.450 he was quite overcome, also alarmed at having so much money, which he said would probably be stolen from him.

In a river bed I once disturbed a pack, which had just brought down a *sambar* hind. It was still alive, its flanks were bleeding from a score of bites, and both eyes had been bitten out. But for the interruption, the pack would have started to eat it, helpless but still alive. I put it out of its misery before I chased the dogs. I counted seven, and was excited at the prospect of collecting so many rewards, but, alas! I was too eager. I brought down one dog and hit another before the pack scattered. I fired at a couple more as they galloped off, but missed both. The second dog I had hit was only wounded, and we had a terrific hunt before we got it. I finished it off with a shotgun. Fortunately wild dogs do not attack humans.

Evelyn was asked to try and procure a couple of wild dogs for a zoo. He told his Forest staff what was wanted, and eventually two half-grown puppies were brought in. We made a cage for them and tried to tame them, but it was hopeless, for they were very savage and quite untamable.

CHAPTER SIX

# Some Leopards, a Man-eating Tiger
# and a Charging Tigress

THE most sporting—and our favourite—way of hunting
tiger is by *ghooming*. We would start out about three in
the afternoon, and wander through the forest on an
elephant, eyes and ears alert for marks on the ground, and
for the calls of animals and birds. We might shoot anything
from a jungle cock to a tiger, it was a question of chance
and jungle craft combined. Often we shot nothing at all,
but we were never dull; it was a joy to be in those marvellous
jungles.

When hunting tiger it is essential to have a good *mahawat*.
An elephant will know at once if her *mahawat* is nervous,
and she will begin to be afraid herself. I say "she" as we
always had female elephants when we were in the United
Provinces. They are much more reliable than the males,
which are treacherous and at times extremely dangerous.

Our elephants were well behaved and staunch to tiger;
they had the odd names of Daisy and Kathleen. We used
to pet them and give them sugar, fruit and bread, but never
anything with an egg in it. I once gave Kathleen a nice bit
of cake. She took it in her trunk, then threw it down, and,
to show her annoyance, she thumped the ground with the
end of her trunk. What they loved above all was sugar cane,
which we could occasionally buy from villages. Their staple
food is the bark of the smaller branches of fig trees. The
branches are cut for them every day by a man called a

*chara-cut*. Each elephant has her own *chara-cut* as well as her own *mahawat*. Every day she is taken to the nearest fig trees, which the *chara-cut* climbs; the branches are piled on the elephant's back, and she walks home so covered with leaves that only her head can be seen. It is fascinating to watch an elephant peeling the bark off the branches with the very tip of the trunk. They do not eat the leaves at all.

When out *ghooming*, or on the march, the elephants browse as they go along, seizing the bits they especially fancy with their trunks. They are careful to clean any earth off roots they have pulled up; they do this by beating the roots against their legs. Elephants have to drink large quantities of water. When we came to a stream we always halted while the elephants drank their fill; they are very particular about having clean water.

One of my favourite amusements was to watch the elephants having a bath. The *chara-cuts* make them lie down in a stream or river. They then scrub them all over with a kind of pumice stone, which the elephants love. When one side has been done they get up, and lie on the other side. At the command of the *chara-cut* they splash water over themselves. Their toilet is completed by painting their foreheads with black paint; this is ornamented in colours with many scrolls and other designs. On special occasions even their toe nails are polished.

An elephant has a few thick hairs at the end of its tail. These hairs are much coveted by Indians for charms; if they get a chance they will try and pinch one or two. Once, when I was on Kathleen, a man crept up behind and tried to cut a hair. Kathleen whipped round so quickly that I nearly fell off, and had it not been for Bisharat Ali she would, I feel sure, have knocked the man down with her trunk. The seeker of charms had a great fright, and I do not think he would ever try that again.

I was out once in the jungle on a strange elephant, which

had been lent to us. Her *mahawat* said he had been accustomed to living in a village and taking his elephant in marriage processions and such-like festivities. He told us that his elephant was afraid of wild animals, especially swamp deer, and as for tigers and leopards she had never seen them, and would most assuredly run away if she did, and she might run for days. We did not believe all this, but I was a little apprehensive the first time I rode on her into the jungle. We had been wandering along for a mile or so, when I heard the alarm call of *langurs*. I could see these great monkeys at the tops of some *simal* trees about 400 yards away on the other side of an open grassy plain.

The ground here was swampy, and the grass was high and heavy. I watched the monkeys through glasses, and saw that they were looking out across the grassy plain. I ordered the *mahawat* to make for the *simal* trees, but he objected, saying that the elephant would run away if any swamp deer were put up in the grass. However, I was determined to go and persuaded him to start. He was obviously frightened, and I prayed that his elephant would not bolt, or he might throw himself off and leave me to my fate.

We had gone half across the plain when there was a commotion in the grass, and two or three swamp deer dashed ahead of us. I prepared for the worst, and imagined myself careering along on a runaway elephant till I was swept off by a branch of a tree. Nothing of the sort, however! The elephant became a little restive, but walked calmly on.

We reached the tree on which the monkeys were sitting, and my eyes searched all round for the tiger or leopard which I knew must be in the vicinity. The *langurs* were scolding and very excited. I could not see anything unusual, so I told the *mahawat* to make the elephant walk slowly around. Part of the plain had been burned and was therefore clear of grass, only the blackened stalks of the tall grass remained.

We wandered about for over half an hour, and I was on the point of giving up the search when the orderly, who was riding behind me on the *katola*, touched my shoulder. He did not point as he had been trained not to do so, but I followed the direction of his gaze, and was suddenly aware of a large leopard walking slowly on the blackened part of the plain towards the jungle. In the leopard's mouth was a female swamp deer, which he had probably killed just before we appeared. On seeing us, the leopard had almost certainly lain flat on the ground, completely invisible to us.

He had nearly reached the cover of the trees and shrubs, so there was no time to be lost. I aimed hurriedly and fired. My shot went a little wide and hit the dead deer, which was blown out of the leopard's mouth. The startled animal jumped backwards in a great fright; he must have thought that the dead deer had suddenly come to life again; he did not appear to connect this queer happening with us in any way. He began to stalk the deer, giving me the chance of another shot. This time I hit my mark, and the leopard bounded off under the trees out of sight.

I asked the *mahawat* to follow him up, but he objected, saying it was dangerous, the elephant would be sure to run away and we might all be killed. However, I insisted, and after a long argument I persuaded him to go forward slowly and cautiously. As I had hoped, we found the leopard lying dead under some bushes, shot through the heart. The elephant was quite calm and behaved very well, which was surprising considering she had such a cowardly *mahawat*.

Just before Christmas, we were camping in the Patli Dun on our way to Jamnagwar, the ultimate home of tiger, where we were having a small shoot. We were sitting by a huge log fire in the Forest bungalow after dinner, when we heard a commotion outside and our orderly brought in a cartman, who was in a terrible state of agitation. He had been travelling in his cart drawn by two bullocks; with him had been a friend from his village. The friend had gone on ahead to cut grass for the animals, and they had agreed to meet at a certain spot on the road. When the cartman reached the appointed place his friend was not there, and he heard groans coming from the jungle on the left of the road. He went a little way into the forest and saw a bundle of cut grass lying all scattered on the ground. He immediately feared that his friend had been attacked by a tiger, although he knew of no man-eater living in these parts. As he had no weapon, it was impossible for him to try and rescue his friend, so he returned to his cart and set off to get help. He had 6 miles to travel before he reached our Forest bungalow.

As it was pitch dark when he arrived, Evelyn decided that it would be useless for us to set out that night. If the man had been attacked by a tiger, he would have been dead for hours before we could get there. We therefore decided to wait till dawn.

We went on two elephants, taking with us the cartman and an Assistant Forest Officer. Arrived at the place, we went slowly into the jungle on the side of the road. We saw the scattered bundles of grass, and then we found some pieces of the man's coat. There was a distinct drag, which we were able to follow; every now and then we found rags of clothing hanging on the bushes, and after about 200 yards we came on the body of the poor man. His lower limbs had been eaten and all his clothing torn off.

The undergrowth was very thick and there was only one small tree suitable for a *machan*, all the others being tall *sal* trees without a branch for 60 feet. The Assistant Forest Officer had never shot a tiger and was eager for the chance, so, although I would have liked to shoot a man-eater, we fixed up a *machan* and left him in it. All this time the tiger was nearby, but, owing to the dense bushes, we could not see him, though we saw the grass moving as he walked through it.

We had not left the spot for half an hour, when the Forest Officer heard the tiger approaching the body of the man, and he became very excited. The footsteps came nearer and nearer, and then he saw the tiger's head partially screened by the leaves of a bush. As he had not had any experience of tiger shooting, he did not wait till he had a sitting shot, and he blazed off when he could only see a small portion of the animal. This was most unfortunate and had disastrous results. The tiger was hit and bounded off, but he was only lightly wounded and he never returned to the kill.

The terrible part was that he lived to kill several more people, and he became so cunning that it was difficult to hunt him. He would make a human kill, eat his fill, and desert what was left. His next victim might be killed 15 to 20 miles away; the whole countryside lived in a state of alarm for many months, until he was finally shot over a buffalo kill by a *shikari*.

We moved on to Jamnagwar. Of all our jungle camps this was the one I loved the best. It was in the wildest and most remote part of the Division, visited occasionally by the Forest Officer, and very seldom by any one else. It is at the head of a valley, the hills on either side are steep, densely forested, and intersected by innumerable branch ravines. The river has a sandy bed, where tigers love to walk. We saw no human footmarks, only the pugs of many tigers.

In those days few sportsmen could reach this inaccessible paradise. The paths leading to it go over steep passes and are too narrow for the passage of carts. Our camels managed to get along, but only just. The camel-men always objected to taking them on this dangerous route for fear they might lose a valuable animal over a precipice.

The bungalow was in a bad state of repair, besides being

*Plate 2 A*
Chara-cuts make the elephants lie down in the shallows, then scrub
them all over with pumice stone, which they love.

*Plate 2 B*
After the bath, the elephants rise to have their toilet completed with
shiny black paint rubbed on their foreheads.

dark and gloomy, but we cared little about that; it was pure joy to be in that wonderful valley.

One evening, after an early tea, we went for a walk, following a footpath which skirted a ravine. Evelyn had his double barrel high velocity rifle and I had the Mannlicher. We had walked about a quarter of a mile along this path, and had just rounded a bend, when we heard the deep bell of a *sambar* in the ravine about 50 yards behind us. *Sambar* being very reliable in their alarm calls, Evelyn walked back, while I waited by the curve of the path so that I could keep him in view. I saw him stop, then raise his rifle and fire. I did not suppose he was shooting at the *sambar*; I knew he must have seen either a tiger or a leopard.

After a few moments I walked slowly along the path and joined Evelyn. He told me he had fired at a tigress, which had been in the ravine below the track. We must have passed within 20 yards and not seen her; she had perhaps been hidden from view behind a tree, and most certainly had been watching us.

When Evelyn fired the tigress had bounded off and had disappeared from view up a side ravine. Evelyn was sure the bullet had gone home. As it would have been extremely dangerous to follow up the wounded animal on foot, we walked back to the bungalow to get an elephant.

We found the camp agog with excitement, as they had heard the shot. It took nearly an hour to saddle the elephant, but the delay was all to the good. If the tigress was badly hit she would perhaps die before we arrived, whereas if we followed up at once she would certainly charge us.

We saw blood where the tigress had been standing, and a trail of it led to a side ravine up which she had disappeared. The elephant went slowly forward; we were holding our rifles at the ready, tense with excitement, and expecting to be charged at any moment.

E

The side ravine led into an amphitheatre surrounded by a steep ridge. The passage became so narrow that the elephant could not get through; we decided therefore to go on the ridge. This meant quite a feat of mountaineering for the elephant. The ridge was very narrow, about 1½ feet broad, the drop on either side being 60 feet or more. The elephant must have felt as if she were walking on a tight-rope!

We had a good view into the amphitheatre, and saw the tigress crouching down ready for a spring. Evelyn fired, and immediately the wounded animal charged with a terrific roar. Our elephant trumpeted, and bolted along the ridge! We could only hold on and hope for the best. With our mount swaying about, it was not possible to get in another shot. It was a most nerve-racking affair altogether, this combination of a bolting elephant, a knife-ridge and a charging tigress.

Fortunately the tigress was so badly hit that she could not charge home. The ridge ended suddenly in a sheer drop, and as we saw this coming we wondered what on earth was going to happen, whether our elephant would go hurtling over into space, or whether she would stop. Elephants are wonderfully sure-footed, also wise, so she came to an abrupt halt. Then the problem was how to turn her round. It was like backing a lorry in a narrow lane, and took much manoeuvring, but at last it was accomplished. All this time the tigress was lying below growling horribly, but fortunately could not move much, so Evelyn was able to finish her off with a well-aimed shot. We loaded her on to the elephant and returned to camp, where we were greeted with much excitement by the servants.

The tigress had a cub, which the elephant men caught and brought to us. We kept it as a pet for a few months; it was quite adorable and became absolutely tame. All the same I was nervous it might scratch someone in play, so we decided the best plan would be to send it to the Lucknow Zoo. This led to a rather amusing incident.

Evelyn's clerk was told to take the little tiger to the railway station and book it off to Lucknow. He came back saying the stationmaster was demanding Rs.200/-, and would the Sahib go and talk to him, which Evelyn did on the following lines:

"Well, Stationmaster, what is all this about Rs.200/-?"

"Sir, a tiger is a wild animal, and my schedule of rates says a wild animal must have a whole wagon to itself, and so the freight is Rs.200/-."

"But Babujee, this is not a wild animal, it is a very tame animal. Let me see your schedule of rates . . . here you are, Babujee, this is a puppy, and the schedule says the rate for puppies is Rs.2/8/-."

"Very well, sir, if you say it is a puppy, I will book it as a puppy." And accordingly it went for Rs.2/8/-!

Shortly afterwards the stationmaster had a more difficult biological problem to solve. A sportsman had found a tortoise and wanted to book it to his home. After frantic searching through his schedule, the puzzled stationmaster failed to find any reference to tortoises, and finally booked it as an insect, and free!

## CHAPTER SEVEN

# Pestilence and Famine

WHEN Evelyn was transferred from the wonderful Division in the foothills we were both very sad; I actually wept. He was appointed Research Silviculturist, and had been especially selected for the job. It meant that he would no longer have his own Division, but would tour all over the Province; we would always be in someone else's Division. The many disadvantages of that were obvious. Worse still, part of his time and work would be occupied with the problems of checking erosion, and afforesting waste lands in the densely populated districts of the Gangetic Plain—Cawnpore, Etawah, Agra and others, far from our beloved forests of the Terai and foothills. In the cold weather, touring in these Plains districts would be very pleasant, and there would be excellent partridge shooting near the big rivers to occupy any spare time. In the hot weather, however, it would be grim indeed, with temperatures up to 120° in the shade and above 100° all night.

That summer two developments occurred that brought unprecedented death and disaster to India. The first was a pestilence that killed ten million people in four weeks! Wells and other imaginative writers have described a world decimated by some new disease. On a smaller scale we saw this happening before our very eyes. There appeared to be no cure; within two or three days the victims were usually dead of pneumonia and heart failure. The medical services were helpless, and anyway not organized for outbreaks of deadly diseases on such a colossal scale. (It was a form of influenza.)

At normal times Hindus take their dead to the burning *ghats* on the river banks and burn the bodies on funeral pyres. But in times of widespread epidemic there is neither time nor material to burn all the corpses, which are just thrown into the nearest running water. It is difficult to visualize the result unless one has actually seen and experienced it.

The Ganges canal is a man-made river more than 200 miles long and 200 feet broad. This great stretch of water, as great as any river in England, was in many places choked with corpses, and gangs of men were employed to break up the jams that formed at every bridge. In one backwater at Allahabad, where the Ganges and Jumna meet, 6,000 corpses were decomposing, to the embarrassment of the municipal authorities. For many months afterwards thousands of human skulls and bones lay glistening on all the river banks. Even the hordes of India's scavangers, the vultures, pie-dogs, jackals, crocodiles and turtles, could not cope with it! Everywhere we went there was an atmosphere of decomposition and death.

The other development resulted from an almost complete and quite disastrous failure of the monsoon rains over a large part of Northern India that summer. Much of the Gangetic Plain is irrigated by canals and shallow wells, where a failure of the monsoon is not an absolute disaster. But in the Agra and Etawah districts and away south to Gwalior, along the Jumna and Chambal rivers and their tributaries, the land is cut up by deep ravines, caused by uncontrolled erosion in the alluvial plain, where irrigation by canals is impossible, and the few scattered wells are up to 100 feet deep. Here a failure of the rains spells FAMINE; but at least the horrors of famine, unlike the horrors of pestilence, can be mitigated to some extent by an efficient administration.

In that year in these ravine tracts there was no rain at all before 21st August, and none after 26th August, and again, no winter rain, so that the unfortunate cultivators lost both their monsoon and winter crops, and it became clear that famine conditions were beginning to develop. When famine is declared the ordinary administration is superseded by the Famine Code—that abiding monument to the British Administration in India.

The basic principle of the Famine Code is to provide food for all the affected population; free for those who are too weak or ill to do any work, but in exchange for work for those who can. Before famine is declared the first operation is to open test works. If these fill up rapidly, the need for famine relief becomes evident.

Scattered about in the ravine tracts there were many experimental areas for ravine reclamation and afforestation, which required soil preparation, and the making of small dams and silt traps, etc., and such operations were considered ideal for test works and famine relief.

Early in March, when famine had been declared in parts of three districts, Evelyn was appointed to organize the reclamation work under the Famine Commissioner. Although, as Kipling wrote, "There aren't many women, sisters or wives, who would walk into a famine with their eyes open," yet it had been done before, and I insisted on doing it again. It was the only time in all our thirty years that Evelyn and I had the opportunity of seeing famine operations and the Famine Code at work. It was certainly pretty grim, but extremely interesting.

It was already furiously hot when we first went down to that "baked Gehenna in the south," and all through April and May it got hotter and hotter, until my diary recorded on 30th May a day temperature of 123°, and 102° at midnight.

The hottest days were characterized by the "*Loo*"—a howling westerly gale straight from the gates of Hell— which continued from 10 o'clock in the morning to sunset. About once a week a sandstorm blew up, depositing red-hot sand through every chink and crevice.

There were about twenty different centres of relief work, scattered over a huge area of ravine desert, that Evelyn had to look after, and which he had to visit regularly. This involved marching from one little bungalow or one-room shack to another, under very different conditions to the marches we had hitherto made in the Himalayas or Terai jungles. To avoid the *Loo* we usually started before dawn, on ponies, camels, or bicycles. I had never ridden a camel before, and, having tried it once or twice, I never wanted to try again. Nasty smelly brutes that jog every bone in your body.

Housekeeping in such conditions was a problem. In that heat, meat and butter were impossible, bread and vegetables were desiccated in a matter of hours, five pounds of ice arrived the size of a walnut, and the idea of ice abandoned for the future. For milk we followed a famous precedent (in "The Day's Work") and acquired some stray goats. Cool water—of which our daily ration was about 3 gallons apiece—was easy; a dozen bottles in a basket of wet straw swaying in the wind. On the same principle the temperature of the living-room was made bearable by *cuscus tattis*, thick curtains made of a fragrant smelling grass, hung over the *open* doors and windows, and kept continually wet.

The organization at the relief works was wonderful. Arrangements had to be made at every centre to accommodate unlimited numbers of men, women, and children seeking relief—at the peak period there were over 30,000 in all—with variable tasks suitable for all. Soil digging for men, clearing brushwood and thorns for women, preparing seed beds for later sowing for children. Quantities of drinking water had to be collected daily in large earthenware pots at every centre.

Every day variable sums were paid in cash, more to each man, less to each child, but sufficient to buy enough food at the Government food depots on the works. Every day cartloads and camel-loads of foodstuffs and grains, fodder for the cattle, copper coins, tools and what you will, came from the distant railheads to every centre.

Everywhere and every day free relief was given to all who were too old or too sick or too feeble or too young to work, also to mothers with babies under ten days old. The Famine Code seemed to provide for every contingency, and we were quite surprised to find one outside its scope. The Code laid down that the mother of a baby actually born on a relief work should get a gratuity of 1 rupee (=1s. 6d.). One dame, who produced twins, asked if she was entitled to 2 rupees. It was decided that the gratuity was not a reward for extra productivity; but anyone with twins in a famine deserved something on compassionate grounds!

The more inaccessible relief works were across the Jumna and Chambal rivers, rising in the Himalayas and the Satpuras near Bombay respectively, and although shrunk by drought, they were still much too wide and deep to ford, and there were, of course, no bridges. So the daily cartloads and camel-loads (as well as ourselves, our servants and our camp equipment) had, when we visited those parts, to be ferried in country boats at various *ghats* and crossings. These are large open boats, which are rowed, or poled where the water is not too deep, by four men, and steered by a fifth. I never saw one which was not overcrowded. An average cargo would include a cart or two, a camel or two, a bullock or two, a herd of twenty or thirty stinking goats, and as many humans as could squeeze on. Every now and then a ferry capsizes, and there is a short note in the papers stating that so many people have been drowned. Fortunately we never experienced this.

As test works and relief works had started early, the famine never got out of control and there were very few actual deaths from starvation. I saw one poor girl, who had struggled in for three days from a distant Native State, so emaciated that she was literally a skeleton under a skin, and her backbone was visible from in front! She died a few minutes after reaching a relief centre. We were saved the horrors of cholera or other epidemics, as most of the people lived in their own villages and came daily to the nearest work, a distance of 2 or 3 miles.

Every day Evelyn would go off before sunrise to inspect one or two works, with a big supply of water, and a wet napkin round his neck. Whenever he came to a river or well, he soaked his shorts and shirt and body with a swim, or a few buckets of water, which gave temporary relief from the scorching heat. But one day when the *Loo* was very fierce, and he and his guide got lost in a maze of deep ravines, Evelyn failed to get back until the afternoon, and frightened me terribly by having heat stroke. As the official report said later: "The work of relief was carried on to the limit of human endurance." I applied the usual remedies, and he was more or less recovered by next morning.

Once a month we had to go to the headquarters in Cawnpore, where we enjoyed the kind hospitality of a big business magnate. In the luxury of his palatial residence with unlimited iced drinks and electric fans (air conditioning had not been invented then) it felt like heaven after the hell of the ravines.

On our last visit to Cawnpore we had left our servants and camp at a small Canal bungalow about 60 miles away, and had gone in by train. On our return our friend, the magnate, to save us a red-hot train journey, very kindly placed his car and chauffeur at our disposal. This was luxury indeed. In those days cars were practically unknown in the country districts off the beaten tracks, and it was something quite new to take a car to the edge of the ravine country.

We started off in the late afternoon, reckoning to get to our destination about 7 o'clock, thus avoiding the heat of the day. All went well for 40 miles along the main road, and then we had to turn off on to a rough district road. We could only go along slowly, avoiding the enormous pot-holes as best we could. A herd of buffaloes was grazing by the wayside. As we came near them they lifted their heads and snorted in an alarming fashion. They looked exceedingly fierce, and so threatening that I urged the chauffeur to step on the accelerator. Evelyn and I seized two sticks, which we brandished, while the chauffeur zigzagged through the deep craters on the road. Suddenly the herd charged, heads down and tails up. I leant over the hood at the back and whacked the nearest buffaloes on their noses, then, with an awful jolt, we crashed into a huge hole and came to an abrupt halt. One big bull charged us from the front, crashing into our radiator, which crumpled up as if it had been hit by a tank. A tiny boy, about 5 years old, then appeared waving a small stick, and the furious buffaloes went off like so many lambs!

With the car thus rudely put out of action, we had now to find some other means of conveyance to cover the 10 miles or so to our camp. Evelyn and the chauffeur went off to a nearby village for help. After much searching Evelyn at last found two possibilities, a camel-cart, and an *ekka*, neither of which we had ever tried before.

A camel-cart is an astonishing piece of antediluvian transport. Imagine an old London horse-bus on a small scale, or a wagonette on a large scale, seating about five passengers on each side facing each other, covered by an arched hood, and fixed on four tiny wheels, with long and very high shafts to which the camel is harnessed. In the late evening, if there is a full load of passengers, the driver sets the camel on a straight 20- or 30-mile course; he then climbs on to the cart and he and all the passengers go fast asleep. The patient camel plods steadily along all night. Next morning the driver and passengers awake at their destination. These carts have no lights, keep always to the centre of the road, and they are a baffling nightmare to the impatient motorist. A friend of ours was so infuriated by one of these carts that he got out of his car, turned the camel-cart round to face the opposite way, and started the camel off. Next morning the driver must have been very puzzled, and he and the passengers very annoyed. Probably the blame fell on a ghost.

We decided in favour of the *ekka*. This is a small platform about 3 feet square above two large wheels, and drawn by a diminutive anaemic pony. The driver sits on the front edge of the platform, one passenger on each side of him, with their legs dangling over the unprotected wheels, and a third passenger can sit cross-legged between them. In wet weather one gets both wet and muddy, in hot weather one gets scorched, and in all weathers one gets shaken to death on bad roads, and very, very tired holding on to something all the time to avoid falling off. It was not an alluring prospect, however; the deciding factor was that the rest of the journey would take about two hours compared to four by camel-cart. We arrived safely without further adventure about 11 o'clock at night.

Early in June the weather changed. The blasting *Loo* ceased to blow, clouds began to form, giving a more muggy atmosphere, and the monsoon was reported to have broken at Bombay. The end of the long drought was evidently approaching, and with it the end of the relief works.

Evelyn had to make immediate arrangements to distribute

to the numerous villages large stocks of seed grain, which had been accumulated, also huge stocks of foodstuffs to give gratuitous relief for three months until the earliest crops could be harvested. Arrangements were made to collect and store and protect from rust tens of thousands of tools and implements, and a hundred and one matters required immediate attention. As soon as the rains came the ravines would become impossible for camels and almost impossible for carts, so that transport on a large scale would cease.

On 10th June, preceded by an appalling thunderstorm, the rains broke with a vengeance. For hour after hour the rain drummed down on the hard-baked barren ravines with astonishing results. Our rest house was on the edge of a deep and long ravine, which had been bone-dry for practically one-and-a-half years. By the evening a raging impassable flood of liquid mud was tearing down past the bungalow; I saw a drowned bullock rushing past.

The relief works stopped abruptly, and next morning not a soul turned up, as all were busy on their own fields and cultivation. We were weather-bound for a few days, and before we left the aching barren landscape had developed a sheen of green; the starving cattle were at last finding a little to eat.

Evelyn was faced with the problem of getting any labour at all for urgent and essential plantation work. Luckily he had an excellent assistant, who worked miracles, and the final results were wonderful.

During the next dozen years the ravine reclamation work continued to expand, and there was one unexpected, and for us very pleasant, development. Grey partridge occur spasmodically through all the ravine country but, in the barren eroded ravines without cover or shelter for their nests and young, their chance of survival is dim. In the plantation areas, after a few years, dense thickets of young trees, and shrubs and grasses produced ideal conditions for partridge nesting, and in consequence they multiplied to an astonishing extent. In course of time the vicinity of these plantations provided the finest partridge shooting anywhere in the Province. I will describe a partridge shoot a few years after the famine.

Early in the cold weather Evelyn was asked to run a one-day partridge shoot for a Government House party consisting of H.E. the Governor, Sir Malcolm (now Lord) Hailey, and two members of his staff. At that time of year the flat cultivated lands, into which the ravines are gradually eating, are covered with tall monsoon crops such as pulse, millet, and corn, dotted about amongst fields of small winter crops, young green wheat, barley, beans, and the like. At dawn the coveys start calling in the ravines, and come out to feed in the nearby crops, to a distance of 200 to 300 yards. Here they stay most of the day unless disturbed, when they invariably streak back to the ravines, where it is impossible to get at them, and they are safe. In the evening towards dusk they return to the ravine areas to spend the night in safety.

These well-established habits of the partridge coveys determined the best way of shooting them, which may be described as a continuous walking drive, L shaped. The long vertical line represents a party of fifteen or twenty beaters stretching out 300 yards into the cultivation. The short horizontal line represents three guns, one at the angle and two in front. If there are four guns, one is put as a back-stop to get a shot at any birds which swing back behind the line of beaters. The guns walk slowly, one in front of the other, along the top of the ravines, keeping time with the line of beaters in the crops.

The shooting party arrived during the night at a convenient railway station; they brought with them two cars and a spaniel. They slept on in their saloons until nearly daybreak, when we joined them. When all was ready, most of us packed into one car, and everything necessary for a large picnic lunch went in the other. We set off for the nearest beat, where the line of beaters awaited us in the dewy crops, and the cool of the morning.

The beat began, and almost at once a strong covey of a dozen or so birds rose in a patch of pulse to an accompaniment of shouts, and swung down over the guns, which banged away merrily, while the line halted. H.E. started off well with a right and left, and a third with his second gun; Evelyn got a couple, but the Staff apparently were not yet awake. Then an odd bird came along, followed after 50 yards by another covey. Then some blue rock pigeon, another covey, and a hare. And so it went on for several miles, with spasms of shooting and spasms of silence, a cloudless blue sky and bright sun above, plenty of good sport and exercise below.

By midday we had covered several miles and most of the plantation in that particular locality. It was definitely hot, and the party was definitely thirsty—it was a moot point whether the Secretary's or his dog's tongue was hanging out further—and as we ended up near the spot selected for lunch we called a halt at the shady tent pitched for the occasion. The beaters received the wherewithal to procure some refreshment, and were packed in a lorry to go about 10 miles to another lot of plantations, around which it was proposed to shoot after lunch, and where we followed them after a refreshing interval.

The afternoon shoot was a good repetition of the morning, but there was one very unusual incident. The spaniel, dashing along through a patch of low scrub to retrieve a dead bird, suddenly yapped, *and disappeared*. When we went up to investigate we heard faint yaps coming (apparently) from the bowels of the earth. He had fallen into an old disused and nearly dry well of unknown, but obviously considerable, depth. It was a problem how to rescue him.

Some of the beaters went off quickly to a nearby village and brought back several lengths of long, strong rope. One of the Forest Guards volunteered to be let down the well and make the rescue. A couple of ropes were firmly tied below his arms, and he was slowly lowered to a depth of about 50 feet, when he called out that he had the dog safely. The bottom of the well was soft damp mud, and by some miracle the dog survived with only a slight shoulder strain; not a bone was broken. H.E. was so pleased that he promoted the Forest Guard on the spot.

My diary records the bag was 156 partridges, a considerable number of blue pigeon, some sandgrouse, and a few hares. Of this total Evelyn estimated that Lord Hailey had contributed more than half.

At the end of the cold weather Evelyn took six months' leave. We both needed a change to a cold climate after the terrible hot weather we had been through.

# CHAPTER EIGHT

## *Tiger Thrills*

W HEN we returned from leave Evelyn was still appointed Research Silviculturist, but we were able to tour in the submontane forests. Evelyn had become tired of tiger shooting, in fact he actually disliked it, which was rather unfortunate, as he had acquired a reputation as a good organizer of tiger shoots. On several occasions he was asked to run shoots for distinguished persons, which he could not refuse to do. On one of these occasions we had a *very* important person in our jungles, and we were exceedingly anxious that everything should go off well. Some of the party were to lunch with us one day, and I racked my brains to think out a really good meal, but, being in the forest, it was not at all easy to get supplies. I wrote to the butcher in the nearest town, some 30 miles away, and asked him to send two fillets of beef, which I planned to have grilled, and served up in small rounds on pineapple and toast. Later I inquired from the butler if the meat had come, to which he replied that something most peculiar had arrived. On the ice he showed me two enormous bullock's legs, complete with huge hooves! I looked at them aghast, and could not imagine what could have happened. There was no time to arrange for anything else, so we had to open some tins. The butcher's explanation was that he could not read my writing very well, and instead of "fillet" he had read "FEET," so he sent two *feet* of beef! The V.I.P. was charming, and highly amused when I told him about it.

I was as keen as ever about tiger, and every other sort of

shooting. An old brute of a tiger lived in the Jaulasal jungles, one of the best blocks for game in all India. He had the unpleasant habit of killing his sons when they were about a year old. We found one of them lying dead with his skull cracked like a walnut by his father's powerful jaws. What would have been a magnificent animal now lying limp and dead aroused my ire, and I decided to avenge him if I could.

A *katra*, tied up at a likely spot near a Terai stream running through thick jungle and cane-brake, was killed on the second night. Cane-brake is a climbing palm (*Calamus* sp.) with shining bright leaves; it looks beautiful festooned about the trees, but it is armed with fearsome thorns, which even an elephant will not face. We had some difficulty, therefore, in following up the drag, but eventually found the carcase. To be able to see it from the trees in which we tied our two *machans*, we had to make the elephants trample down the surrounding grass and shrubs. We sat up from 3 o'clock till dark, but the tiger did not turn up, though we knew he was about, for a *sambar* was calling in alarm some way off.

Next morning Evelyn woke up feeling very ill, having eaten something which had poisoned him badly. He could not possibly sit up in a *machan*, so I had either to go alone or lose the chance of shooting the tiger. I decided to go, though Evelyn never liked me to go alone, in case something unexpected happened.

The tiger had been back in the night. He had eaten a large meal and dragged the remains into dense cane-brake, so that we had great difficulty in finding the carcase. I chose a place for my *machan* high up a tall tree, so high that I had a struggle to reach it on a rope ladder. My own ladder had been mislaid and I had to use a makeshift one, the rungs of which had been spaced so far apart that I could hardly stretch my legs from one rung to the next.

F

I was hanging in mid-air swaying about, and despairing of reaching the *machan* at all, when suddenly a *sambar* gave an alarm call quite close to the tree. This meant the tiger was coming, or at least that he was on the move.

An orderly was sitting in the *machan* steadying the ladder, and two men were holding the end near the ground. One man came up and pushed hard at my behind, while the orderly leant over and made frantic grabs at my shoulders. Their united efforts at last succeeded in getting me to my seat, where I felt quite giddy, and wondered how on earth I would ever get down again. I hastily screened myself with leaves while the orderlies untied the ladder and departed. The elephants had cleared a space round the carcase, which I could see plainly.

A *sambar* belled once or twice, which kept me on the alert. Presently I saw a tiger's huge head appear, followed by his massive shoulders. He was sniffing hard at the elephant's footmarks, and then he raised his head to smell at the bushes that had been cut back. He was evidently suspicious that something unusual had taken place in his absence.

When my heart had quietened down, and I could hold the rifle steady, I took a shot at his neck where it joined his body; it was exposed to view, as his head was lifted right up. I fired, and knew I had not missed, but the tiger bounded off as if unhurt, and silence descended on the jungle. I waited for half an hour before shouting to the *mahawats*, who were some distance away. They brought up the elephants, and I climbed down the rope ladder on to one of their backs. As it was nearly dark I went straight back to the bungalow.

Next morning Evelyn had recovered sufficiently to accompany me to look for the tiger. We saw fresh marks on the road, so Evelyn at first thought that I must have missed, but, on closer scrutiny, we saw the pugs were those of a tigress. We both prayed that the tiger was not wounded, or we might look for serious trouble in the cane-brake. I began to feel nervous, and I wished I had never shot at the brute. We followed the direction I had seen the tiger take, and, to our immense relief, we found him dead 50 yards from where he had been hit. The tigress had found her dead mate, for we saw her marks all round him. The next day or two she roared in the jungle, lamenting her dead spouse but, as he was such a nasty old brute, she was well rid of him.

The reader must not imagine that a tiger lurks behind every bush in Indian jungles, and that one has only to mount an elephant and go out and shoot one. Even in the finest jungles in all India, as the U.P. submontane forests unquestionably are (with an average total bag of 100 tigers every year), weeks and even months might pass without seeing a tiger, although seldom two days pass without seeing signs of them.

There is, of course, a great deal of luck in tiger shooting. I mean in small personal shoots, not the big affairs run by Maharajas and Princes, where vast beats are organized and much money is spent. For instance, the main thing, when sitting over a kill, is to get the tiger to return for a meal while it is still light enough to see to shoot. It is a question of luck, assuming that all necessary precautions have been taken, whether the tiger happens to be hungry. Sometimes a tiger has already made another kill; which he will want to finish before starting the new one. In this case he will hide the fresh kill carefully, and may not return to it for several days; meantime the impatient sportsman sits up wearily and sees nothing. If he is on short leave he may have to return to duty before the tiger comes back.

It is also a question of luck if one can find a natural kill of a deer or a pig. A natural kill offers more chance than that of a buffalo that has been tied up as bait, for the tiger, having killed his natural prey, will be less suspicious.

Jaulasal was one of our favourite hunting grounds. The forests here are on the last ramparts of the Himalayas, which are steep little hills broken up by many side ravines, and the hills gradually peter out into flat grassy plains called *chaors*, which are surrounded by dense forest. Thousands of deer of all sorts feed on the *chaors* at night, living in the forest in the day. Tigers and leopards prey on the deer. In the evenings we could hear the alarm calls of the different deer, marking the passage among them of the large carnivora. Often too we heard the reverberating roar of a hungry tiger, or the sawing call of leopards. It is a wonderful forest.

One evening Evelyn and I went out *ghooming* into the forest bordering the *chaor*. We rode on the famous elephant Balmati (from whose back F. W. Champion took some of the wonderful photographs which illustrate his two books). We saw several *sambar* hinds, which stood gazing at us, not at all alarmed; they were used to seeing wild elephants, and quite possibly did not notice the *katola* with us seated on it. There were deep ravines running through the forest, some of which we had difficulty in crossing, but, with Bisharat in charge, I was never nervous. If the descent were very steep, Balmati would squat on her hind legs, and toboggan. On a sharp ascent she would use her trunk as a fifth leg. It was sometimes difficult to hold on while clutching a rifle, but I used my legs as well as my hands, gripping the post of the *katola* as one would the pummel of a saddle.

We were going through a thicket of clumps of bamboos when Balmati halted, and I noticed that Bisharat was looking directly ahead. I followed the line of his gaze, and for a few moments could not make out what was attracting his attention. I was looking for a tiger or perhaps a leopard, but I was startled to make out the form of a huge tusker elephant. His grey colour merged into the background so perfectly that he was invisible, which sounds absurd, but so it was. The tusker had his trunk lifted in our direction and his great ears were pricked forward. He was only 30 yards away.

Now all *mahawats* are afraid of wild elephants, and even brave Bisharat did not like them, especially tuskers, which might molest a tame female. If he did attack, we should be in a very dangerous position, so the only thing to do was to beat a hasty retreat. Bisharat made Balmati back a few steps, and then he turned her, and urged her to her fastest pace—in fact, we fled. I watched the tusker, which took a few strides after us with his trunk uplifted, and I thought we were for it, but fortunately he stopped, and we were soon well away. Elephants are protected in the United Provinces, and may not be shot.

We went on through the forest listening for calls. Soon in the distance we heard the alarm calls of *chital*. We hastened in their direction hoping it was a tiger that had alarmed them, and not a leopard. Bisharat drove Balmati as hard as he was able, but the ground was broken, and we had to negotiate some nasty places. We feared that the *chital* would stop calling before we could reach them, but at last we saw some of them and slowed down. We were now on the edge of the forest; in front of us was the bare *chaor*. On our left a small copse ran out into the *chaor* for a little way like a peninsula. We hunted about for some time but could not see anything; the *chital* had stopped calling, and we feared our quarry had moved away.

We knew that a tiger or leopard would never leave the cover of the forest and go into the open *chaor*, so we did not even look in that direction. The only place left was the small copse, and, although we thought it an unlikely place, we went in to have a look round it. We were advancing slowly, both holding our rifles ready, when Bisharat stopped the elephant and held her steady. No one spoke, and I looked for either a tiger or a leopard, I did not know which, but I was certain that one of them was visible.

For a moment or two I could not make out anything, neither could Evelyn, but Bisharat, with his keen eyes, had spotted a huge tiger, and he continued to hold Balmati steady with a gentle pressure on her forehead with his *gudjbar*. Suddenly Evelyn saw the tiger, and he realized he had not a moment to lose. The immense beast was crouching low, with his head on his paws preparing to spring at us. His tail twitched slightly, which was what had attracted Evelyn's attention. Evelyn aimed carefully at the tiger's huge head, and mercifully his bullet went true, and the great beast rolled over, shot through the brain. Evelyn gave a great sigh of relief, for he knew full well that had he missed, or wounded the tiger, the infuriated animal would have charged at us, and he could easily have jumped up on to the elephant. He was the biggest tiger we ever shot, measuring 10 feet 3 inches between pegs.

Tigers do not usually attack elephants, but we had cornered this one on the peninsula of forest surrounded on all sides by open plain, except for the narrow neck on which our elephant stood. Thus the tiger had either to break into open country or charge us. Evelyn had not fired a moment too soon. We realized afterwards that it was one of those moments when we had been in very great peril, but Providence looked after us.

The tiger was very heavy, and we wondered how the four of us (the fourth being an orderly) would be able to load it on the elephant. Nearby was a bank to which we dragged the carcase. Bisharat ordered Balmati to kneel down below the bank and lean over towards it, then with ropes, which we always carried with us, we pulled the tiger over the edge of the bank on to her back. Many elephants will not allow a tiger to be loaded on to them, but Balmati had been perfectly trained and she did not object. Evelyn and I walked home, Bisharat drove Balmati, and the orderly sat on the tiger.

I hope the reader will not think that we were very cruel and bloodthirsty. I looked at our shooting from the point of view that tigers and leopards do a great amount of damage to herds of buffaloes and cattle, and therefore a certain number of them have to be shot to protect the villagers from heavy losses of animals. Many villages and cattle stations are surrounded by forests and grassy plains, so that if carnivorous beasts were allowed to multiply unchecked, any livestock the villagers possessed would have a poor chance of survival. Cows out of milk are left to wander on the grassy plains, often without a herdsman; they find their way back to the villages and cattle stations at night. If any are missing a search is made, which will probably end in the discovery of a half-eaten carcase hidden under a bush, or in heavy grass. The tiger or leopard responsible for the kill may be lying up nearby, and he will roar his annoyance if anyone approaches too near. Even if a man is with the herd, he cannot protect the animals without a gun or rifle. His only weapon being a stick, all he can do is to shout, which would hardly be sufficient to intimidate a tiger. If any sahib is in the neighbourhood the herdsman will go to him for help, and beseech him to come with his rifle and slay the marauder.

Often and often men have come to us for assistance, and whenever possible we have gone back with them either to sit up in a tree over the kill, or to search around on an elephant hoping to come across the tiger.

There was one pathetic old man who came to us with tears streaming down his wizened old face. He told us that he was a very poor man, his only possessions had been five buffalo cows. These animals had been grazing on the grassy plain, when they had been attacked by a tiger and tigress. All five had been killed, and he could have done nothing to save them. He was ruined, and I felt desperately sorry for him.

It is unusual for tigers to kill more than one cow or buffalo at a time, but sometimes a tiger will run *amok*, as they say in India, and he will kill just for the fun of it, or it may be to show off his strength to a tigress. We went with the old man and we shot the pair of tigers; the tiger from a *machan* and the tigress from an elephant. We gave the wretched man some money, but it would take him years to recover the price of five cows. To shoot that pair of tigers was not cruel, but a just retribution.

Our orderlies were adept at skinning animals and curing the skins, which they pegged out and preserved with wood ashes and alum. Owing to their skill we never had a pelt go wrong. The skinning had to be done immediately the carcase was brought into camp, especially in the hot weather, when to leave it unskinned, even for one night, might ruin the skin. If we came in late the men had to do the work by the light of one or two lanterns. When skinned the carcase was carried by the sweeper (man of low caste) outside the camp, where next morning miraculously assembled vultures would pick it clean in a very short time. Sometimes villagers and coolies would ask for strips of tiger meat to act as charms. We had to guard jealously the whiskers, claws and lucky-bones, or they would all have been taken. Just as whales have tiny atrophied leg bones, so tigers have small atrophied collar-bones, and it is these that are thought to be lucky.

Some Americans, who were shooting with us on one occasion, wanted to eat a bit of every animal and bird that they shot. They ate some tiger, some bear, some leopard, and many other animals; they then suggested that they should try some vulture. Evelyn, horrified, hastily told them that vultures were holy birds, and on no account must they be shot.

Our orderlies were as keen on *shikar* as we were ourselves, probably more so. They loved to boast how many tigers their Sahib and Memsahib had shot, and every incident would be highly embroidered. When I missed a tiger or any other game, I felt quite ashamed and apologetic. They were a fine lot of men, mostly from Garhwal. In those days their pay was pitifully small, amounting to about 10 rupees a month, but they had no hard work to do, they enjoyed their official position, and were proud of their smart uniforms provided by Government. One man I remember well, his name was Bansi. He started as my dandy coolie; with three other men he carried my sedan-chair up and down the hills of Naini Tal, being always obliging and cheerful, making himself useful about the house, willing to do any odd job. He was delicate, and the really strenuous work of carrying a dandy uphill was too much for him. In the rains he went down with pneumonia; he was desperately ill, at death's door. I looked after him, made him a cotton-wool jacket, and saw that he was nursed properly till he recovered. As soon as he had a vacancy Evelyn appointed him to be our orderly, and eventually he became a Forest Guard. He was always our devoted friend.

CHAPTER NINE

# Fight to the Death

WE CAMPED sometimes at Tanakpur on the Sarda river, one of the major rivers of the Himalayas. Where it debouches from the hills, the river spreads out into a mile-wide bed of boulders and sand, dotted with islands of *shisham* trees and coarse grasses. Tanakpur is a small townlet situated about 60 feet above the river. It has a railway terminus, a bazaar and several small bungalows, which are situated on a high bank looking over the wide river bed. Across the river are the dense forest-clad hills of Nepal. A ferry goes to and fro, used chiefly by Dhotial coolies, who live in West Nepal. The ferry is no more than a hollowed-out tree trunk, which will take six or seven men.

One afternoon Evelyn and I crossed the river in the ferry and landed in the forbidden land of Nepal. Two fierce Gurkha sentries came up to ask who we were and to bar our further advance. Evelyn offered them cigarettes, which calmed them down, and we had a friendly chat before we embarked on our return journey. We little guessed then that, years after, we would live in the mysterious kingdom of Nepal for seven long years.

In the cold weather Tanakpur is a busy market town alive with hill people. Forest contractors export large quantities of timber from the extensive forests. Farther up the river is a timber boom to catch logs floated down from the hill forests. In the rains Tanakpur is deserted. The climate is extremely unhealthy, so bad that the entire population

90

leaves; the hill people go back to the hills, and the forest contractors go to their homes in the plains. The flooded river cuts off all communications with Nepal.

Late one evening, when we were staying in the Forest bungalow, we were watching three men fishing with nets in the waters of the Sarda. Suddenly two tigers and a half-grown cub emerged from one of the grassy islands close by. We heard the men shout, whereupon the tigers moved off across the dry bare bed of the river towards the forest on the right bank, a quarter of a mile away.

Simultaneously we heard from this forest the trumpeting of a wild elephant, and soon after the terrifying roar of a charging tiger. We got our field-glasses, and were astonished to see a big male tusker elephant come out on to the bare river bed, being furiously attacked by two tigers.

Spellbound we watched this titanic battle, which raged up and down the river bed in full view of the bungalow. Presently it grew too dark for using field-glasses, but the moon rose, and we could still watch the fight. The noise was appalling. The elephant trumpeted and bellowed, the tigers roared hideously. About 11 p.m. the noise died down and the tigers disappeared.

Next morning we found the elephant lying dead at the foot of the bank just below the bungalow. There was no sign of the tigers. We examined the marks on the elephant. The trunk was quite untouched, but both eyes had been clawed out, and there were deep scratches round the eyes. There were terrible bites and scratches on the top of the head and neck, back and rump, and the throat had been torn open—evidently the *coup de grâce*.

We wondered what could have provoked the tigers to attack the elephant. It is inconceivable that they made a senseless and unprovoked attack on a full-grown tusker, and equally inconceivable that the elephant started the fight. It is probable that the tiger cub was the cause of the trouble.

He may have blundered into the elephant and received a kick which made him yelp. The tigress's maternal fury would have been aroused, and she would have come to the help of her cub; the tiger would have joined in the affray.

It was interesting to note how the wounds on the tusker indicated the tactics of the two tigers. It was evident that no frontal attack had been attempted, or the trunk of the elephant would have been mauled.

We surmised that one tiger had threatened in front, enabling the other tiger to leap on the elephant's back and start biting and scratching. At some stage of the battle one of the tigers must have managed to crawl on to the top of the head and scratch out the eyes, perhaps deliberately, for it seems a natural instinct of the cat tribe to go for the eyes.

The poor elephant, blinded, had staggered on, tortured with the fiendish laceration of his back, stumbling along in agony over the boulders of the river bed, falling at last over some obstruction, and exposing his throat to a fiendish mauling by the other tiger, finally dying from loss of blood, or severance of his windpipe. The tigers had taken a terrible revenge for any possible injury to their cub. The tusks were small and looked old.

Evelyn had a consultation with the Ranger as to what should be done with the carcase. It was not possible to dig a pit deep enough to bury it in the river bed, which was full of boulders. The Ranger employed a gang of coolies to collect boulders, and this being accomplished, they built them up in a huge cairn round and over the carcase. This, however, proved to be a failure. An appalling stench came through, and jackals and stray dogs managed to creep between the stones, and pull out pieces of flesh.

Evelyn decided that the only thing to do was to try and burn the whole thing. The Ranger poured about 100 gallons of kerosene oil over the body, and made a huge bonfire of the dry driftwood from the river bed. He then set fire to the funeral pyre, which burned for several days, by the end of which time only the bones and the skull of the tusker remained.

# CHAPTER TEN

# *Dacoits*

THE dense forests of the United Provinces are a good hiding-place for any who have committed crimes and wish to evade the police. Sometimes bands of armed robbers, called *dacoits*, live in these jungles and, from their hiding-places there, they raid villages and attack travellers on the roads.

There was one well-known *dacoit*, called Sultana, who defied the police for many a long day. He and his band lived in our forests, not always in the same district, but covering a very large tract of country. If our Forest Guards discovered the lairs of the *dacoits* they could not be expected to betray them, for they knew that if they gave information to the police their lives would be forfeit. The *dacoits* probably gave them money to keep them quiet.

The robbers were armed with ancient guns, swords and knives. Their method was to attack a village at night, killing anyone who offered resistance. Usually the villagers were too frightened to oppose them, and the *dacoits* would tie up the men before systematically searching the houses for money and valuables, which they took off, sometimes on pack ponies if the haul were big. One or two women would also be taken, bound and gagged, and kept in the forest for their pleasure. Sultana was something of a Robin Hood. It was said that he robbed rich travellers to give some of their money to poor beggars and needy folk.

When we were marching through forests frequented by *dacoits*, we were nervous for the safety of our string of baggage camels. As the *dacoits* would have risked a good deal to get hold of our guns and rifles, we were careful to keep them with us on our elephants.

We were camping in the Ramnagar Division near a forest known to be frequented by *dacoits*. There was no bungalow there, so we had to live in tents. When I told Evelyn that I was nervous that our camp might be raided, he pooh-poohed my fears, saying the robbers would never dare come near us. All the same I did not like it. One is very vulnerable in tents the doors of which cannot be even closed, let alone locked, and it is easy for anyone to creep under the canvas walls.

Evelyn had a summons to headquarters, and I was left alone in the camp for several nights. I kept a loaded gun by my bed, and I arranged booby-traps all round the tent—brass basins propped against the doors, tin cans and tin tubs put against the walls, which would be knocked over if anyone tried to crawl in. I kept a night-light burning by my bed. I must confess I slept very badly and was thankful when dawn came.

The next night, after arranging my booby-traps, I was not quite so nervous and soon fell fast asleep. Suddenly I was awakened by an awful clatter of tins; seizing my gun as I leapt out of bed, I prepared to defend myself, my heart was thumping so hard that I could scarcely breathe. I could not see anyone, and soon realized that a wind had sprung up, which had caused my booby-traps to fall down. It was a false alarm! Evelyn roared with laughter when he returned and I told him about it.

When Evelyn was in the tent with me I forgot my fears and slept soundly. One night something woke me from a deep sleep. The night-light was burning by my bed, but when I sat up to look around I could not make out anything unusual in the dim light. I had a torch under my pillow but, being very drowsy, I felt too lazy to switch it on. I was just dropping off to sleep again when I heard soft footsteps, which I imagined to be those of a stray dog outside the tent. I shouted, "Hat jao (Get out)," turned over, and went to sleep again. Evelyn had not wakened at all.

Next morning when Evelyn got up he could not find any of his clothes. "They must be there," I said, "look on the floor."

I got up and noticed at once that everything had gone off the dressing-table, my suitcase was also missing. Then I remembered the footsteps I had heard in the night, and I knew a thief had been in the tent. When I had sat up and looked around, he must have been hiding behind a chair, so that I had not noticed him in the faint light. We came to the conclusion that it was not wise to have a light in the tent, which enabled a robber to see what he was doing, and helped him to avoid falling over boxes and chairs. It was not pleasant to think that this man had probably been creeping about in the tent for some time. If I had seen him, and raised the alarm, he might have attacked us with a knife, and we would have been easy victims, so perhaps it was just as well I failed to notice him. We thought he was probably one of Sultana's gang.

Evelyn warned all his contractors about the *dacoits*, advising them to hide all their money and valuables, which they promised to do. They sometimes have large sums of money in their camps, for they have to pay their sawing gangs, cartmen, etc.

One day Sultana and his gang raided a contractor's camp, but found little of any value. They took all the grain and food they could find, but there was no money in the huts. Sultana was a cunning rascal; he thought out a plan. He and some of his men went off to the Range quarters, where the Forest Ranger lived with his family. The Ranger was captured, also a Forest Guard, the womenfolk were locked up. The Ranger and Forest Guard were forced to take off their uniforms and were then securely trussed, and locked in the Range quarters.

Sultana dressed himself in the Ranger's uniform and one of his men put on that of the Forest Guard. They then went off to a big sawing camp, followed at a distance by the gang, who hid in the jungle, while Sultana, dressed as the Ranger, accompanied by the pseudo Forest Guard, went boldly into the camp.

The contractor, suspecting nothing, greeted Sultana, who explained that the other Ranger had been transferred, and he had been appointed in his place. He said that he had come to give warning about Sultana and his band of *dacoits*, who were known to be in the neighbourhood. The contractor replied that he had taken precautions, and had hidden all the money and valuables. Sultana said he would like to see if the hiding-place were a safe one, whereupon the contractor showed him where he had dug a pit and covered it over with piles of timber. Sultana blew a whistle, the gang rushed up, overpowered the contractor and his men, and went off with many hundreds of rupees.

The contractor came to Evelyn in a great state at the loss of so much money. The Ranger was badly frightened, besides suffering from a sore head and bruises. Evelyn, of course, reported the matter to the police, but by the time they arrived Sultana and his *dacoits* had moved off, no one knew where. Between raids the robbers often returned to their villages, where they worked in the fields for a time.

My sister Sybil came to spend a few weeks with us; she wanted to sample camp life. I enjoyed having visitors in the jungle, it was nice to have someone else to talk to except just ourselves. Evelyn is a man of few words, he can and will talk only of things which interest him, such as philately and geology, whereas I longed to gossip of more mundane subjects. I remember a dinner party at Government House

G

when we very junior folk. Evelyn, as usual, was sitting silent, and I was watching him, when suddenly I saw him burst out laughing. He told me afterwards that the lady on his left had turned to him and said, "Wah, wah, wah, we must say something; I see the Governor's wife looking at us with displeasure!"

But to go back to camp. We were staying at a small Forest bungalow in a very remote and lonely part of the Division. There were just three rooms—a living room with a bedroom on either side—the house was gloomy, hemmed in on all sides by the forest. As was our usual custom in camp, we had gone to bed early. At about midnight we were awakened by piercing screams from Sybil's room. We leaped out of bed and raced across the living room, falling over furniture in the dark.

My first thought was that somehow a leopard must have got into Sybil's room and must be mauling her, or perhaps she had seen a snake or had been bitten by one. It is amazing how quickly ideas flash through one's brain. We collided with her in the doorway and she told us what had happened.

She had been asleep, but something had awakened her, and feeling her bed-clothes slipping off on to the floor, she had half sat up to pull them on again. As she did this she almost bumped noses with a man who was crouching by her bed! She had screamed and made a grab at him, but he eluded her, making a dash for the bathroom door, which he had some difficulty in opening. Evelyn roused all the servants, but it was pitch dark and there was nothing to be done.

We thought it probable that the intruder had been hiding under the bed when Sybil retired for the night. There was only one window, which was covered with mosquito-proof wire, and the door to the bathroom was closed, and could not be opened without making a clatter. Next morning we traced footmarks to the edge of the forest, and we guessed the man was one of Sultana's followers.

About this time Government appointed a special officer to hunt down the *dacoits*; his name was Freddy Young, famous in United Provinces for his ability and his size. He opened an intensive campaign, with his spies in many villages, and soon learned from them that the robbers were in a certain part of the forest. He organized an encircling movement, hoping to round them all up.

He divided his forces into three companies commanded by himself, another Police Officer, and Evelyn; there were altogether about 300 men. It was a very dark night when they all set out. The plan was to attack from three different directions and encircle the stronghold of the *dacoits*.

In the darkness the party of the second Police Officer missed the way in the jungle and became entangled in a morass of cane-brake, thus leaving a gap through which the gang escaped. However, much of their equipment was captured, including guns and ammunition. Sultana had had a fright and for some time he and his men disappeared.

One day Evelyn was inspecting a plantation with the Ranger and some Forest Guards when they came on a party of men who were carrying bundles on their heads and guns in their hands. When they saw Evelyn and his small party they threw down their bundles and fled, closely followed by Evelyn, the Ranger, and the Forest Guards. Evelyn tripped over a tree root and fell headlong, so he was out of the chase. The *dacoits* turned and fired several shots, but fortunately their aim was not good. The Ranger, being unarmed, had to retire. A small village had been raided, but the robbers got nothing worth having.

Freddy Young was soon on the scene. At last Sultana realized that he could not evade capture for much longer. He therefore sent a message, through his spies, that he would like to meet Young Sahib and have a talk with him.

He stipulated that the Sahib must come unarmed and absolutely alone to a certain remote spot in the depths of the forest. There he would be met by two men who would guide him to the inner sanctuary of the band.

Freddy was a man of iron nerve so, courageously, he agreed to the proposal, and set off on the appointed night unarmed and alone. When he reached the spot, two men, armed to the teeth, stepped from behind some bushes and tied a bandage over his eyes. They then marched him off, leading him by the arm.

Freddy said that they seemed to walk a very long way, sometimes struggling through heavy grass, at other times pushing through thorny bushes, which tore his clothes. At last they halted. When the bandage was taken off his eyes he saw that he was surrounded by fierce-looking men, all heavily armed, pointing their guns straight at him.

Sultana stepped forward, salaaming. He said that he and his men would agree to go back to their villages and give up their dacoities if the Sahib, in the name of the Government, would promise that they should all go free and not be punished.

It was not possible for Freddy to agree to this. He realized, from the glowering looks of the men, that his life was in great danger; some of them wanted to shoot him then and there, but Sultana restrained them. He said he had given his word that no harm should befall the Sahib, and he would not go back on it. The bandage was once more placed over Freddy's eyes, and he was escorted through the forest to the spot where he had entered it.

As is often the case, Sultana was finally caught on account of his infatuation for a woman. It became known, through the spies, that Sultana was in the habit of visiting a woman in a certain village, so watch was kept and one night her house was surrounded, and Sultana was caught at last. He was taken handcuffed and chained to Bareilly, where he was duly tried and condemned to death for the many murders he had committed.

When he was in the condemned cell awaiting execution, Sultana asked if Young Sahib might be allowed to visit him. Sultana pleaded that, when his followers had been eager to kill the Sahib, he had saved him from them, now it was the turn of the Sahib to save him, and he begged the great Sahib to have mercy. Freddy Young pointed out that the matter did not rest with him, so Sultana, the great *dacoit*, paid the penalty for his many crimes.

## CHAPTER ELEVEN

# The Hailey Park*

As Evelyn grew more senior he became a Conservator, and finally Chief Conservator. Instead of only a Division to inspect, he had the forests of the whole Province to control, which meant that we had to do a great deal of touring, besides keeping up a residence in Lucknow, where he had to attend Government conferences. I had always looked forward to the time when Evelyn would be at the top of the tree entitled to wear, on State occasions, a coat embroidered with gold lace, knee breeches and buckled shoes, but when he had reached this exalted position I realized that a Divisional Forest Officer has far the best life. His Division is his own little kingdom, where he reigns supreme, except for a few weeks every year, when his Conservator comes round to inspect. These weeks are either enjoyable or the reverse, depending on the Conservator. We had some charming ones, others were a sore trial.

Evelyn was able to do a tour in the Ramnagar Division, and the Patli Dun, again visiting our beloved haunts of bygone days. Joined by Bill, our elder son, who had travelled from Burma for a month's leave, we spent our silver wedding in this wonderful valley. Bill had joined the Forest Department in Burma, being the third generation to have chosen forestry as a profession.

A few years earlier when Lord Hailey was Governor of the United Provinces, he announced at a meeting of the U.P. Game Preservation Society that 150 square miles of

* Now called Corbett Park.

this tract would be made into a Game Sanctuary. Evelyn was asked to demarcate the sanctuary, and draft an act for the Legislature. When this was passed in due course, the Hailey National Park was created. The rigid exclusion of all shooting and even carrying of firearms, had an astonishing effect on the wild life, and the creation of motorable roads has made relatively accessible the innermost parts of the Park and doubled the possibilities of seeing wild animals. For it is far easier to approach within a few yards of deer, and even tiger, in a car than on foot, since animals have no instinctive fear of a car as they have of Man himself. I saw seven tigers in nine days by day from our car, one so close that I could nearly touch it through the window! All day and every day in the Spring great herds of *chital* are out grazing on the grassy plains, and dozens of little hog deer haunt the banks of the river.

We spent a never-to-be-forgotten month fishing, and roaming in the jungles looking for game to photograph. Bill was very keen on photography, and having shot two tigers when he was with us on a previous visit, he did not want to kill any more. He said he would far rather take their photographs than have their skins.

It was a beautiful morning when, mounted on Balmati, we went out into the forest to take some pictures of animals. Off we went hoping that the proverbial luck of beginners would counterbalance the heavy odds against our being able to approach within photographic distance of a *sambar*, or any other animal, in a place with sufficient light for a good picture. We had not gone far before we saw several hog deer, but they were shy, running away with heads held low whenever we tried to get closer. A little farther we saw a number of *chital* hinds crossing a branch of the Ramganga river—a charming sight but, as usual, we were too far away to try a photograph.

Balmati continued sedately on her way, now and then

plucking a tuft of grass with her trunk and fastidiously dusting it against her front legs before placing it in her mouth where it was chewed with exemplary slowness. Suddenly Bill was prodded in the back by the sharp-eyed orderly, who was sitting behind, and following his gaze (talking and pointing not allowed) we saw two *chital* stags with horns in velvet, both very fine heads. They had not seen us and were standing broadside on, facing away from each other, a magnificent picture if only we were 15 yards away instead of 50. Bill pushed the *mahawat* gently on the shoulder, and Balmati moved slowly towards the stags but they soon saw us and, after a long stare, they took fright moving off with horns held flat along their backs. We followed for about half an hour before losing them completely. Once we succeeded in approaching within 15 yards but, unfortunately, they were in dense thicket and a photograph was out of the question. At last we had to give up, without getting a picture of what are possibly the most beautiful deer in the world.

We continued to *ghoom* and presently saw a *sambar* stag with a moderate head walking across our front. He was not as shy as the *chital*, which enabled us to follow him for some time exposing a number of films but, owing to the distance and the lack of light, the negatives obtained proved to be not worth keeping. Eventually he joined a party of two hinds, one stag with horns about 12 inches long and one young one. We approached them very slowly and got within about 20 yards, but they were under some shrubs, and did not show up well on the focusing screen. They evidently decided that we were harmless, and continued to graze, while we stood still, wondering what to do, when the stag solved the problem for us by leaving the party and starting to walk across our front. The *mahawat* grasped Bill firmly by the foot to call his attention.

Now was his chance, for the stag was just coming into

*Plate 3*

Two *sambar* hinds, after a long stare, decide that our elephant is harmless, and continue to graze in the shade of the forest.

the open. The camera was hastily focused while he emerged from the bushes and stood for a few seconds gazing at us, perhaps puzzling at this strange combination of elephant and men. Balmati lived up to her reputation and stood rock-still, thus enabling Bill to take the chance of a lifetime. With trembling fingers he released the shutter; our beginner's luck had held! The light was now failing, we had been on the elephant for three hours, and it was long past tea-time, so we turned Balmati homewards.

From the bungalow we had a fine view over the pure forest of *shisham*, which here covers the wide valley where we had been wandering all the afternoon. The fresh leaves were just sprouting and we looked over a sea of beautiful apple-green, reminiscent of an English beech wood in Spring. In the distance the hills of Garhwal were tinged a pale grape-blue in the fading light. We were enjoying the peaceful scene and listening to the murmur of the Ramgamga below us, when there came up out of the valley the long moaning call of a tiger on the prowl, a wonderful and unforgettable sound.

# CHAPTER TWELVE

## *Life in Kathmandu*

To look forward to anything too much is a great mistake and so often leads to disappointment. For many years I had longed for the time when Evelyn would be able to retire and we would live in the house of my dreams in England, but the War broke out and my plans, like those of countless others, were shattered.

Evelyn took up an appointment in Nepal, where he could do something to help the war effort by organizing supplies of timber.

We journeyed to this strange and mysterious country, and so different was our life that we might have arrived on another planet. We had had no idea what conditions would be like, but the whole world seemed to be breaking up around us so we did not worry much about anything, and only prayed that we would win the war.

When we arrived in Nepal the country was actually neutral, and three Germans were living in Kathmandu. They were ostensibly looking for minerals but it was believed that they were engaged in other activities. The British Minister pressed for their removal and, finally, the Maharaja agreed to expel them, but being neutral he would not arrest them, leaving that to be done at the frontier.

At first we felt very strange. We had not imagined that we should have to attend so many State functions, which are exceedingly formal. When we were sorting our belongings before our journey Evelyn could not find room for his morning suit (which he had had since we were married), so light-heartedly I gave it away to the bearer. On arrival we found it was the one suit that was absolutely essential. Evelyn must wear it whenever he had an interview with His Highness or any of the Commanding Generals, in fact he had almost to live in it. We had perforce to send measurements to Calcutta and get one immediately at a very high price.

I started off with a bad *faux pas*. His Highness very kindly sent us a present of fruit and vegetables, so I sat down and wrote a letter of thanks beginning, "My dear Maharaja, Thank you very much for the lovely fruit you so kindly sent us, etc.," and continuing further with more yous and yours. After the letter had gone I was told I must not use the personal pronoun at all when speaking or writing to His Highness, but I should have written, "Thank Your Highness for the lovely fruit Your Highness, etc." I asked the British Minister if I should write an apology but he advised me to leave it, as His Highness would understand it was a mistake.

At first the State functions were an agony to me. We had to arrive at an exact moment; it was impossible to arrive after one person or before another. The British Minister, His Highness and his Majesty arrived last of all, in that order. On alighting from our car we would be confronted by a large crowd of Commanding Generals, Generals and Colonels, and with each Commanding General and General we had to shake hands in strict order of precedence but we must never shake hands with the Colonels. They did not help by coming forward themselves so that for a complete stranger it was very difficult to remember which General was senior, I even found myself trying to shake hands with a Colonel who prevented me by firmly holding his hand behind his back!

The Commanding Generals and Generals looked magnificent in their fine uniforms and many of them were exceedingly charming, but it was difficult to get to know them well in the few fleeting contacts we had at these functions. The policy was "no fraternization with Europeans," so we could do little more than smile at each other well apart. Senior Commanding General Sir Mohun (afterwards Maharaja) was especially nice and always showed us the greatest kindness.

Durbars were very formal affairs. His Majesty, dressed in a smart uniform blazing with orders and wearing his magnificent jewelled hat, a glittering mass of diamonds and huge emeralds, would sit on the throne. His Highness the Maharaja would do homage to him, followed by the Generals all in resplendent uniforms and superb hats covered with jewels, each with a sweeping plume of Bird-of-paradise feathers. When this had been done the few Europeans (in those days only eight) would each be led up in turn and presented to His Majesty; the men bowed, the ladies curtsied. The Generals and Colonels sat on either side of the Durbar Hall which was very long, with a parquet floor; from the ceiling hung some magnificent crystal chandeliers. It was somewhat of an ordeal to walk hand in hand with the Maharaja past all the nobility.

Occasionally evening Durbars were held, which were even more splendid and formal. The European ladies wore full evening dress and long white gloves; sometimes at these evening functions the four European ladies were taken to see Her Highness and the Court ladies who, of course, never appeared in public. Some of them were extremely beautiful, with very fair skins and lovely features. They wore exquisite saris of delicate hues, embroidered with precious stones and pearls; their tiaras, necklaces and bracelets were dazzling. I used to think how much more becoming a lovely sari is than European evening dress. The Court ladies would have boxes and cupboards full of these beautiful saris, each one worth a small fortune. There was not much we could talk about in the few minutes we had together; our children and the weather being the usual topics. I would very much have liked to know these delightful ladies better. All the Generals had big palaces, beautifully furnished, where they lived in great splendour. Their wives visited each other, but they must have had very few amusements shut off from the world as they were.

Life in Kathmandu was never ordinary or humdrum. Things seldom went according to plan, in fact we seemed to live in a turmoil of crises. Evelyn had many difficulties connected with his work and found it difficult to reconcile himself to the guiding principle in Nepal that everything is of value *except Time*: I often wondered how he kept sane; he used to wake up early, then lie awake composing the most bitter and sarcastic letters to the Government, some-times he even went so far as to write them. He invariably tore them up, but several times a year we debated whether he should hand in his resignation. Having so little society and being so isolated from the world outside, we worried over trifles, and often made mountains out of mole hills, a state of mind for which we coined the word, "Nepalitis."

Housekeeping in Kathmandu was a headache. I had to think months ahead to ensure a supply of everything we needed. My store-room was like a shop with shelves full of tins and bottles. Tea we ordered in 20 lb. chests, sugar and flour came in 80 lb. sacks. We made our own bread with a yeast obtained from the Salvation Army in Lahore. Evelyn is fond of crumpets so, knowing very little about it, I tried to instruct the cook how to make them. Our first efforts were not very good, but Evelyn nobly ate them. We tried again several times, and were congratulating ourselves that our crumpets were nearly perfect.

That evening I found Evelyn on the floor in the drawing-room; he was scarcely able to breathe and said he was feeling his heart. Terrified I sent for the Doctor Babu, and with the help of the servants helped Evelyn upstairs. The Doctor Babu listened to Evelyn's heart and looked very grave. I asked what we should do, to which he replied that all we could do was to massage the heart. He then rushed round to the British Minister to warn him that he considered that Evelyn was desperately ill. The news, of course, spread like wildfire all over Kathmandu, and next morning the Maharaja sent his own doctor, an Indian. By this time I was feeling extremely worried and prepared for the worst. However, the Indian doctor was reassuring. He said that the condition of the heart was caused by pressure due to indigestion. He prescribed some medicine which soon gave relief. That is the last time I have ever made crumpets!

Our chief amusement was golf on the 18-hole links on a grazing ground five miles out along a ghastly road. It was a good natural course but very rough. The greens were small round patches of cut turf, the hazards were mostly deep ravines over which we had to drive. We usually had the whole course to ourselves so there was no need to hurry. We each had two caddies; one to carry the clubs, the other to go in front and mark the ball—a fifth caddy carried the flag ahead to each hole. The total cost of the five boys would be about 1s. 6d., and this only if no balls were lost on the round.

The links were not far from the famous temple of Pashupati, where all devout Hindus in Nepal would like to die. Often when playing golf, I would see corpses tied to a pole and covered with a cloth, or on a bed, being taken to the burning *ghats*; once or twice I saw men not yet dead, but dying, being carried along so that they might die with their feet in the sacred stream. Behind them walked a relation carrying a load of fuel for the funeral pyre.

When we went out to play golf we often took our butler along to boil a kettle for us so that we could have a picnic tea at the ninth hole. We could never eat the meal in peace for hordes of brown monkeys would lie in wait, ready to dash on to the tablecloth if we relaxed our vigilance for a moment. The view from the links was enthralling, many high snow peaks were visible. Gauri Sankar (23,440 ft.) stood out well, Everest was just hidden by another giant nearer to us. At sunset we would watch entranced as the pink glow crept up the mountains and we were able to note which were the highest peaks. When the last faint tinge of pink had faded the mountains looked as cold and lonely as death.

We sometimes went for picnics to various places in the valley but these were usually spoiled for us by leeches. These horrible creatures infest the jungles and the grass, they are even to be found in the bushes from where they drop on you as you pass. We wore white shoes so that we could see the leeches better and we carried bushy twigs with which we beat off the invaders. We always carried small packets of salt, nevertheless it was impossible to avoid the leeches. If one stopped for a second on a path one would see hordes of leeches advancing from all directions. Sometimes I went along in a series of bounds and jumps but, in spite of everything, I usually collected several of these disgusting torments. The small kind is bad enough, but the large cattle leeches are quite terrible, two or three inches long, and when full of blood a repulsive sight.

Our Goanese cook, who had been with us for 20 years, was miserable in Kathmandu. He was a Roman Catholic, about the only one in Nepal; there were no others of his race and he was completely cut off from female society. To have had any relationship with a Nepalese woman would have meant imprisonment, if discovered. He had always been a man of moods but now he showed signs of becoming unbalanced altogether.

In the evenings we used to sit in the drawing-room with the windows wide open and curtains undrawn; it was far too warm to shut up anything. As I sat reading, or doing my tapestry, I would become conscious of someone outside the window looking at me with great intentness. I could just make out the face of the cook looking from the corner of the window-sill, and there he would remain for a long time, probably unaware that I could see him. This happened again and again till I became quite worried.

Once Evelyn had to go away for a few days, and I was left alone in the house. All the servants lived in outhouses some distance away. As usual I was sitting reading on the sofa after dinner when, looking up, I saw the cook standing just behind me. I had not heard a sound and do not know how he had entered the room so noiselessly. As it was most unusual for him to come into the house at that late hour I was considerably startled, but tried not to show it. I asked him what he wanted and he replied that he felt lonely. He then sat down, and I talked to him in Hindustani for a little while about old times and Bill, whom he remembered as a small boy.

After 10 minutes or so I got up and told him to go, which he did much to my relief. Subsequently I found him several times creeping about the house; on suddenly opening a door I would find him just outside or he would emerge from behind a curtain. Finally we decided he had better go so we found him a good post in India but, after so many years, I was sad to see him depart, and we missed his master hand in the kitchen.

We had a *masalchi* (second table servant and washer-up) who was a Kasai. He was looked on as a bit of a wag by the other servants. He had a wife and two children. One day we found out that they had taken up their abode in one of our fowl houses made of mud and grass, which measured not more than 8 feet by 4 feet 6 inches. This we could not allow so we had to evict them. His pay was enough to keep them comfortably, but he drank heavily; not that he was

*Plate 4B*

Typical Newar handiwork. A stone figure outside a temple at Patan, Nepal.

*Plate 4A*

Pagoda-style temple in Bhadgoan. On each side of the steps are stone figures of giants, elephants, and dragons.

ever drunk, but he consumed three bottles of country liquor a day and in this way wasted all his money.

One morning two policemen came and arrested him. We learned that he had been caught in the act of selling cartridges, which he had stolen from us from a box we kept unlocked in Evelyn's dressing-room. It was amazing how quickly the authorities got wind of the matter. The offence was a serious one in Nepal, and though Evelyn pleaded for leniency he could do nothing to help the wretched man. We were distressed to hear that he had been beaten severely. He was tried and sentenced to two years and three months imprisonment, but actually he was released after a few months, perhaps owing to Evelyn's solicitude. His miserable wife and children were left to starve, but we took pity on them and provided food. We asked for permission to re-employ him when he came out of prison but this was refused. We therefore put on the small boy of six to look after our chickens, and paid him the wages we had formerly paid his father, and thus the family was saved from beggary.

Our happiest times in Kathmandu were when we had Bill with us on leave from Burma. Before he came we had to obtain permission from His Highness, who very kindly gave him a permanent invitation to visit Nepal. We had one or two other guests and would have liked to have many more, but permission was hard to obtain and often refused.

Red Cross work occupied a great deal of my time. We did what we could to raise money for this cause and other war funds. Evelyn made sets of Nepal stamps, which he sold for the Red Cross, and the sale of Nepali jewellery was organized and brought in quite a big sum. This junk jewellery, made of silver set with turquoises, coral and other semi-precious stones, became very popular.

In the cold weather, from November to April, we toured in the wonderful forests of the Nepal Terai where we were

H

completely happy and glad to get away from the formalities
of Kathmandu. We travelled into very remote parts, some
of them not visited before by Europeans. My only worry
was that the forests are extremely unhealthy, and in the case
of illness we were completely cut off from any medical aid.
Cholera and smallpox are endemic and there was always the
danger of typhoid and malaria. On his first tour Evelyn
went without me as he wanted to find out what conditions
were like. He disappeared into the blue and I had no letters
or news of him for a month. I then had a message saying
he was ill and was being carried out on a stretcher to
Raxaul, the railway terminus of Nepal. When he arrived he
looked ghastly, but fortunately there was an excellent
European doctor at the Mission on the frontier who looked
after him. It was a bad attack of malaria.

About once a year we went to Calcutta where I thoroughly
enjoyed the shops and cinemas. At the end of one visit, I
had done so much shopping that I had a number of packing
cases to take back with me. I bought a ticket for Raxaul at
a travel agency and went to the station about ten minutes
before the train was due to leave. To book my boxes, I had
to produce my ticket; I searched for it in my bag but could
not find it. Owing to the black-out it was very dark in the
station but, look for it as I might, I could not find the
ticket. It was swelteringly hot and, as I became more and
more confused and bothered, large drops of perspiration
splashed on to the platform from my heated brow. Finally
the official, who was waiting for the ticket said, "Madam, it
is no use looking for your ticket, as you have lost your
brain!" At this I burst out laughing and I laughed until I
nearly had hysterics. I am sure the official thought I was a
raving lunatic! The train left without me and I had to
return with my boxes to the hotel for the night.

Next day I went to the travel agency to ask if they could
issue another ticket, which they said they could not do

unless I paid the whole fare again. As it was quite a considerable amount I decided to try to find my lost ticket. I had the loan of a car so in this I rushed round to all the shops where I knew I had been the day before. It took some time, as in one shop they took up the carpet and in another they turned out the dustbin, but in the very last shop I had visited I found it. It had been picked up on the floor and must have fallen out of my bag.

The train journey from Calcutta to Raxaul on the Nepal frontier is a nightmare. I left Howrah station at 8 p.m. with my bearer, Azmat, and piles of luggage. I had a holdall in which I had blankets, sheets and pillows. Azmat made up a bed for me on one of the long seats, which on Indian trains run up and down the carriages, and not across as on English trains. The lines have a gauge of 5 feet 6 inches, so there is plenty of room to be quite comfortable. Each compartment has its own lavatory and wash-basin; there are no corridors, one is completely cut off from the rest of the train. To go to meals one has to alight when the train stops at a station and walk on the platform to the restaurant car.

Before the train left Calcutta I made a thorough search of the carriage and the lavatory. I have heard of cases where thieves have hidden under the seats and attacked a lone passenger when the train is in motion. A friend of mine, attacked in this way, struggled bravely with a naked and oiled thief who overpowered her, but he was subsequently caught and identified by marks on his back where she had bitten him!

Satisfied that there was no one hidden in my carriage I bolted the doors and windows and lay down, but I could not sleep. The train rattled along raising clouds of dust which penetrated the wire windows and nearly choked me. My face, my hair, my hands, everything was covered with dust. Every now and then we drew up at a station with a bang and a clatter. Vendors of tea, biscuits and what-have-you rushed up and down the platform shouting and banging at the doors of the train. "Tea for Hindus." "Tea for Muslims." "Cigarettes, Pan, Water," they cried. Third-class passengers, who wished to board the train, rushed about wildly looking for places where there were none to be had in the already packed carriages. Not being able to read that mine was a First-class compartment they kept trying to open the door. At one station I rashly lowered a window to see where we were; a beggar tried to climb in and, to my horror, I saw that he was a leper. I yelled so loudly that the guard heard and came to my assistance.

At midnight we arrived at Mokameh Ghat on the Ganges. Here we had to leave the train, to cross the river on a steam-boat ferry. As the train drew up at the station the passengers poured out on to the platform in a yelling screaming mob. They jostled and pushed each other in their frantic efforts to get first on the boat, but why there was such need of haste I could not understand. I had learned by experience that I must wait till the first rush was over. The first time I did the journey I did not know this, consequently I was carried along with the crowd and at times swept off my feet. My hat was knocked off and I was terrified that my handbag would be snatched from me. As we approached the gangway on to the ferry I was very nearly pushed into the river. It had been a most alarming experience.

This time I sat in my carriage waiting for Azmat to bring coolies to carry my luggage. It seemed a long time before I saw him pushing his way through the crowd looking very worried. He told me that he had given his bundle of bedding and a small box to a coolie, but in the confusion he had lost sight of him and he could not find him anywhere. I asked a Police sepoy to help us, but it was obvious that the coolie was a thief and there was no hope of catching him.

When I arrived on the boat I was quite exhausted. I left Azmat to look after my boxes while I had some tea in the refreshment room on board. I had some plum cake with me, and I ordered tea and sandwiches. A tall good-looking European came in and sat opposite me at the table. As he only ordered a cup of tea I offered him a sandwich, for he looked desperately tired and pale. He almost grabbed the sandwich and I realized that he was very hungry. He proceeded to finish the sandwiches, also the cake, and while he ate he told me about himself.

He had been in a Scotch regiment stationed in India and he had fallen in love with a Eurasian girl. He had not been allowed to marry her while he was in the regiment but, when he returned to Scotland and got his discharge, he had spent his gratuity on the fare back to India so that he might marry his sweetheart. He had obtained a job as guard on the O. and T. Railway but his pay was so little that it was impossible for them to live in European style.

One day he had seen an advertisement in a Calcutta paper for recruits for the Calcutta Police Force and he immediately made up his mind to apply. As far as Mokameh Ghat he could travel free but from there to Calcutta he must pay. He had hardly any money so he could only afford a Third-class ticket. Arrived in Calcutta he had an interview and was told that he must have a medical examination two days' hence. He had no money for a lodging and very little for food. He walked about Calcutta for two nights and a day with an occasional rest on the Maidan. The third day he passed his medical examination and was accepted for the job. He had travelled back to Mokameh in a Third-class carriage, and I knew well what hell that must have been for a European. His last few annas he had spent on the cup of tea.

From Mokameh Ghat the train loiters along stopping at

every tiny station. On the platform there are always terribly diseased beggars and mangy dogs but by this time I had such a headache that I could hardly see. The Legation Rest-house at Raxaul in its shady garden seemed like Heaven when I arrived there at tea-time.

# CHAPTER THIRTEEN

## *Peoples of Nepal*

DESPITE its limited size and population Nepal provides a most astonishing ethnological complex. In a population of 6,000,000 a score or more languages are spoken, all mutually unintelligible. Even in one valley one village may speak a language which the next village cannot understand.

The reason for this amazing complex of races and languages is that the primitive aboriginal (Dravidian) inhabitants have been overlaid and enslaved by two waves of invasion; by Mongolians from the north and east, and by Aryans from the south and west, and were largely driven into the malarious and unhealthy Terai and jungles of the outer hills, which the invaders could not tolerate, but pockets of the aborigines have also survived here and there.

The Dravidian aborigines arrived before historic times. Julian Huxley has recorded that about 6000 B.C. Neolithic Man started the cultivation of cereals in the foothills between Palestine and Persia. Compared to the earlier hunting stage which had lasted half a million years, this agriculture led to a relatively rapid increase of population and for the next 2,000 years waves of Neolithic culture spread from these foothills to Mesopotamia and the Tigris, to Egypt and the Nile, to India and the Indus, and possibly along the Himalayan foothills.

It was at first an economy of small villages, possessing the following characteristics: Neolithic man had domesticated a number of animals, had developed cultivated strains of various grains, could brew fermented liquor, weave and spin, and had developed a primitive religion for inducing and maintaining fertility.

These characteristics have survived to the present day amongst the aboriginal tribes of Nepal, and in many cases no new characteristics have been evolved. One wonders what it is that keeps one tribe or people unchanged for 8,000 years while another contemporary tribe develops into the Atomic Age? For that matter, what kept the little shell Lingula unchanged for untold aeons of time while its contemporaries developed into Primates and Elephants?

During our extensive wanderings we came across many of these aboriginal communities, who had never seen, or been seen by, Europeans, and we gazed at each other with mutual interest. One small but very interesting tribe was even more primitive than Neolithic Man as the people had no land or cultivation and no dwellings or fixed abodes. These were the Bhotes of the Chitawan Valley, who live on and by the Gandak river, catching fish with nets and harpoons, hooks and traps, using dugouts with supreme skill, and supplementing their diet with wild fruits and edible roots. They build themselves tiny temporary huts of grass and reeds on the river beaches; they migrate up or down the river in their dugouts as the spirit moves them. In one respect, however, they are in advance of their Neolithic ancestors as they extract traces of gold from the river sands, which they barter for their iron hooks and spears, and so are not dependent on bone and stone.

A little higher up the primitive scale are tribes like the Musahirs (i.e. "Rat-eaters") and Sunthals, who have their settled villages and primitive cultivation, but still depend largely on their bows and arrows to supplement their diet.

Higher, again, are tribes like the Dhimals and Raj-bansis, who cultivate rice extensively and also keep domestic animals, poultry, etc. They are neither Hindus nor

*Plate 5 A*

"Ten thosand miles on elephants" - or quite a lot of them-were travelled as shown in this snapshot. Crossing a river in the Nepal Terai

*Plate 5 B*

The aboriginal Sunthals have primitive cultivation, but depend largely on their bows and arrows to supplement their diet.

Buddhists, but believe profoundly in spirits and ghosts, both good and bad, and go to considerable trouble to propitiate them. Their little villages are mostly in clearings of greater or less extent in the Terai forests. We could not, of course, talk with them, as neither my Hindustani nor Evelyn's limited Gurkhali was of any use, and no one understood their language anyway.

While the Aryan invaders were pouring into India from Iran through the north-western passes—somewhere in the second millenium B.C.—the Mongolian emigrants were pouring in from Tibet through the northern passes and, roughly speaking, the latter occupied the northern, central and eastern tracts of Nepal, while the former (at a later date) found themselves in the southern and western tracts.

If legend and folklore are to be believed, three different races in Nepal to-day are of mixed Aryan and aboriginal origin. There are first the Newars of the valley of Kathmandu. They may have migrated from the north, or the legend may be true that they came to Nepal with Buddha and liked it so much that they settled there.

Before the rise of the Gurkhas around A.D. 1750 there were three petty Newar kingdoms crowded into the Nepal valley with their capitals at Kathmandu, Patan, and Bhadgaon, all of which are profusely decorated with pagoda-style buildings, temples, carved wood, stone and metal work for which the Newars are famous, and which now make these ancient towns so picturesque. Newars were employed as skilled workmen in Tibet, Tartary, and many parts of China.

Some of these temples are decorated in a style that looks very odd and indecent to Western eyes. There is, for instance, a small square temple in the middle of Kathmandu bazaar, which has six panels on each side, and each panel shows a man and woman together in different attitudes. Evelyn once asked his Assistant about the origin of this temple, and received, in reply, the following fairy story, or

bit of folklore: Long ago the inhabitants of the Valley were
very simple and ignorant about sex and reproduction. So,
as they were gradually getting fewer and fewer, the Gods
took pity on them and built this temple to show them.

Newars are mostly Buddhists, but seem equally at home
in Hindu shrines and temples, and they take part in Hindu
festivals. There was one sinister sect (whether Newar or
Hindu I never discovered), who lived in a village near
Bhadgaon, and dressed in long white robes. Once every
12 years they chose a young man of their community, gave
him a royal time for 12 months, and at the end of that time
drugged and killed him, dried his flesh, and stored it in a
particular temple for 12 years to provide food for their local
deity. Without this sacrifice, it was firmly believed that
utter disaster would befall the whole valley, therefore it was
expedient that one man should die for the people. At least,
that is the story we were told. In recent years this practice
has been forbidden, but our Assistant said it still went on.

The second race of mixed origin is the Dotials of north-
west Nepal. They are well known at every hill-station in
the Himalayas, where numbers of them migrate yearly to
earn money as porters and weight carriers. They carry loads
on their backs held in place by a rope attached to a band
which goes round their foreheads. They are exceedingly
dirty people, usually dressed in woollen coats made of a
patchwork of rags, and long trousers, tight round the legs,
and very baggy round the waist. They have long hair
matted with grime and they wear small round hats. On their
feet they have sandals with rope soles, or they go barefoot;
they have a peculiar shuffling gait. They have very little
intelligence, and know only a few words; they are, in fact,
human beasts of burden. It always pained me to see them
staggering along under their terrific loads, some of them
mere boys. They earn more money than ordinary coolies as
they can carry so much more, but they wear themselves out

and die young. As they shuffle along, many of them spin the wool with which their clothes and blankets are made.

The third race of mixed origin is the Tharus of the Terai, who are practically immune to the deadly malaria prevalent in that tract. According to Northey, in the 12th century high-caste Rajput women from Chitor in Rajputana escaped to the Himalayan foothills and when, after some years, it appeared that their husbands had been killed, they began to take husbands from among the aboriginal inhabitants of the Terai, and their offspring became the Tharus. They are not found west of the Sarda river nor east of the Bagmatti. They are very fine *mahawats*, good cultivators, and they keep their villages scrupulously clean, a rare characteristic in India.

As a result also of the Moghul invasions, some high-caste Thakurs and Rajputs, who were driven out of Central India, took refuge in the Himalayas and from these high-caste immigrants have descended the Ranas and nobility of Nepal.

Within the past few decades there has been quite an extensive influx of traders and shopkeepers, Marwaris and Banias, and even a few Muslims here and there to add to the galaxy of communities and races that make up modern Nepal.

Turning to the Mongolian invasion, the centre of the country is largely occupied by the four Gurkha castes or sects, i.e. Gurung, Magar, Rai and Limbu, who prior to 1947, were extensively recruited for the 20 (and in the war up to 40) battalions of the Gurkha regiments of the Indian Army. They are so well known throughout the British Empire, and indeed the world, that many people call the inhabitants of Nepal "Gurkhas," whereas the true Gurkhas form but a small proportion of the whole. As army pay and pensions were their main support and livelihood it must have been a shattering blow to this sturdy, virile, cheery race when the independent Indian Government after 1947 stopped all recruitment except for the few battalions still employed by the British, e.g. in Malaya.

Gurkha villages lie predominantly in the zone between 4,000 feet and 8,000 feet, the limiting factors being the prevalence of malaria below, and increasing snow and cold above. Gurkha women are comely, they love to adorn themselves with massive silver ornaments and many strings of brightly coloured beads. They are expert knitters; I once saw a woman knitting with the spokes of an old umbrella. She was overcome with delight when I gave her some real knitting-needles.

The higher altitudes are populated almost entirely by tribes of Mongolian origin—if we choose to ignore the Abominable Snowman. In the north-western part of Nepal, the boundary between Nepal and Tibet swings northwards, away from the main crystalline axis of the high peaks, and in this part, e.g. Mustang, the climate, the country, the inhabitants, are almost indistinguishable from Tibet proper. Farther to the east we find at the high altitudes the Lepchas, and the now famous Sherpas, whose assistance is so essential in all high Himalayan expeditions.

I have mentioned 15 or 16 different peoples; that does not nearly complete the list or make a pretence of being exhaustive but it does, I hope, dispel the idea that all Nepalese are Gurkhas.

One of the most remarkable features of Nepal life is the enormous extent of annual or seasonal migrations, and all on foot. (Wheeled vehicles, except in the Terai, and in or to Kathmandu, are non-existent in Nepal.) Large sections of the population with nothing else to sell, sell themselves for manual labour. Every year tens of thousands of hillmen leave their homes in the late autumn to work as grass-cutters, timber-carriers and sawyers, in the adjoining sub-montane forests of India, trekking down 7 or 8 days' journey to the nearest railway station and returning again in March. Similarly thousands of Dotials make the long journey to the hill-stations as far away as Simla. Gurkhas, going and coming, used to be a constant feature of the crowded hill roads, which were made still more congested by the tens of thousands of pilgrims visiting or returning from the sacred temples and shrines making trips that sometimes took several months.

Some hill villages do have some produce for sale and it is carried in thousands of large baskets on thousands of human backs, for journeys of several days to a week or more. Oranges, guavas, turmeric, chillies, for example, are thus carried. Endless streams of loads of hand-made paper, slabs of timber and firewood can be seen coming daily into Kathmandu from villages often a week's journey away. To add to the general crowd, Tibetan traders come over high passes with flocks of sheep and goats, each animal carrying a load of borax, salt, wool, skins, yak tails, or other queer things, accompanied by fierce Tibetan dogs, which are trained to spend all night and every night barking to scare off leopards.

# CHAPTER FOURTEEN

## *Nepalese Customs*

MARK TWAIN, the American humorist, once wrote a fantasy of the imagination to which he gave the title "A Yankee at the Court of King Arthur." Since we lived in Nepal there has been a revolution and great changes, so the contents of this chapter apply to an epoch that has passed and conditions may be very different now. But in 1940 it was no fantasy of Mark Twain's imagination, but conditions in many ways were quite as fantastic; conditions that had come down with little change from the times of Shahjehan, of Solomon, of Cyrus the Persian! Nowhere else in the world had the absolute and personal rule of an oriental potentate survived as in this secret and closely-guarded land of Nepal, which had kept at bay for generations all modern ideas of equality, fraternity, liberty, democracy and the like. It was less than two decades since universal slavery had been abolished and the slave mentality was still prevalent.

The Constitution then might be described as an unconstitutional Monarchy, ruled by a hereditary Prime Minister. His Majesty the King, descended from Prithwi Narayan, the conqueror of Nepal in the 18th century, was the titular figurehead without power or authority. There was a certain amount of friction at times between the followers of the King and the followers of the Ranas, as the following rather astonishing incident illustrates.

Some ringleaders of a party bitterly opposed to the Ranas hatched a plot to kill them and their principal supporters. I don't think the ringleader was called Guy Fawkes, but it would have been a most appropriate name! The plot, briefly, was to fill the cellars below the King's cinema with gunpowder and to blow the place up the next time the Ranas came to watch a film.

Large numbers of kegs of explosive were obtained from Calcutta, which were sent up to Kathmandu on the Ropeway. Unfortunately for the plotters one of these kegs broke open at the terminus spilling its contents in the Customs House, which led to an investigation and the seizing of all the other kegs. A Court of Enquiry was held which decided that the King himself could not possibly have known of this wicked and dastardly plot, and all six of the ringleaders were condemned to death by hanging. To discourage future plotters, the sentences were carried out with the maximum of publicity. The condemned men were taken around the streets and avenues of the town in a lorry, which stopped here and there under a big tree; one of the condemned, with a rope round his neck, was then taken out and strung up to a branch where he was left dangling for two or three days, as an awful warning. One man tried to escape; he jumped out of the lorry and, being a fast runner, he eluded the sepoys for a time, but the rope tripped him up and he was recaptured.

The corpses hanging from the trees were a terrible sight. We could not avoid seeing them as they were in the main streets of the town. Evelyn reminded me that only two or three centuries ago similar scenes were of frequent occurrence in the heart of London. Did not Guy Fawkes himself provide one of them?

The 1950 revolution has changed all that. It makes quite dramatic reading how the King escaped from his palace, to take refuge in the Indian Embassy. He was flown out to Delhi as the guest of the Indian Government and later he returned in triumph with the powerful support of Pundit

Nehru, replacing his infant grandson who had been proclaimed King in his absence, and replacing also the all-
powerful Rana family, which had ruled Nepal for a hundred
years.

An attempt was then made to introduce into Nepal a
modern democracy with a Prime Minister and Cabinet,
universal adult suffrage and the rest, words and ideas that
convey no meaning whatever to the medley of wild illiterate
tribes and communities that compose Nepal. It is impossible
to replace an oriental despotism suddenly by a modern
democracy and the attempt was given up. The administration is now in the hands of His Majesty the King, assisted
by a Council of Ministers appointed by him.

The founder of the Rana family was a great character
called Jung Bahadur Rana who, about 1850, abandoned a
job of catching elephants to become Prime Minister,
supreme Commander-in-Chief, and Maharaja, with all the
power, authority and wealth of Nepal in his hands. After
the Indian Mutiny of 1857 Jung Bahadur went to England
as a guest of Queen Victoria; he stayed at Buckingham
Palace, which so impressed him that one day he astonished
the manager of a big west-end business by ordering a
replica of the palace complete with similar furniture,
pictures, etc., to be erected in Nepal! The result was the
great Singha Durbar, an oriental version of Buckingham
Palace in Kathmandu, with mixed oriental and mid-
Victorian furniture, which we often visited.

Landor records a story of Jung Bahadur which shows he
was much more than a wild illiterate elephant catcher. At
a gala performance of the opera, which he was obviously
enjoying immensely, Queen Victoria asked him how he
enjoyed it so much without being able to understand it.
"Madam," he replied through the interpreter, "I also enjoy
the songs of your wild birds like the nightingale, although
I do not understand them."

*Plate 6 A*
The famous Buddhist temple of Bodhnath, visited yearly
by thousands of pilgrims from Tibet and even China.
The eyes of Buddha look over the valley.

*Plate 6B*
In the valley of Kathmandu a typical Newar carries his children in
baskets, followed by another with garden produce.

Jung Bahadur created the Nepal Constitution which survived for 100 years. The Kingship was to be hereditary—from father to son—while the post of Prime Minister and Maharaja was to pass to the eldest surviving (legitimate) male of the Rana family, i.e. to the next brother, or possibly nephew, thus eliminating the risk of putting a weak minor in supreme power.

The authority of the Maharaja was absolute. Every phase of policy, every law and decree and *sanad*, every petty or major appointment, every small or large item of expenditure, had to be decided and approved by the Maharaja. All Government appointments, both civil and military, were for 12 months, to be renewed yearly as the Maharaja decided.

The control of expenditure, urgent or petty, left subordinates no option or initiative—sometimes with ridiculous results. There was the case of a Government Treasury 300 miles from Kathmandu the thatched roof of which accidentally caught fire. Instead of putting out the blaze the Treasury officer sat down and wrote a report, asking for Rs.20 to be sanctioned to put it out. The report went by post-runner, i.e. on foot, over unbridged rivers and high mountain passes at 10 miles a day reaching Kathmandu a month later. Here it stuck for another month in the bottle-neck that habitually surrounded the supreme power, and finally the sanction was received three months after the fire had burnt down the building! This little example illustrates how things worked in Nepal when we were there.

The Director of the Forest Department had a remarkable knowledge of English. One day, when Evelyn was more than usually exasperated at the dilatory work of the office staff, he burst out, "Their work is like the Peace of God . . ." The staff beamed at the compliment that they were like a "piece of God," but the Director smiled, and later remarked to Evelyn, "You meant their work . . . 'passeth all understanding.'"

I

As Evelyn was a European many of the rules were modified in his case. If he had embezzled Rs.10,000, or made a bad contract, or incurred expenditure not approved, he would not have been held personally responsible *but his Head Clerk would*, a hereditary liability even to the third generation! It speaks well for the high reputation of British officials in India that there were no lack of candidates for the job. And, of course, the liability never arose.

The system of filing and official correspondence was unique in our experience. Such things as typewriters, duplicating or calculating machines were unheard of. (When Evelyn asked for a stenographer he was told there was no such thing in the Kingdom.) Letters, reports and the like were written by hand in Hindi script on small pieces of hand-made paper about 10 inches square, and no copy kept. When the first square of paper was full, a second similar piece of paper was stuck on to the end and then a third and a fourth, and so on. Thus a file grew longer and longer with age, and was rolled into a fattening cylinder for convenience. An average file required a whole room to see the beginning, a big file necessitated study in our drive, the record file (it is said) was $1\frac{1}{2}$ miles long, and required the parade ground for perusal.

If a file was lost there was no record of it or its contents, so the matter would be forgotten. An accused man had been convicted by a magistrate in a distant town and condemned to death; his file was sent to Kathmandu for confirmation of the sentence. The man's friends arranged a mail robbery *en route*, the papers were destroyed, the case forgotten. Prison sentences were quite severe for some crimes. One of the worst crimes was to kill a rhinoceros for which the penalty used to be 75 years' *hereditary* imprisonment! (But this was given up when slavery was abolished.)

When a Maharaja died or abdicated there was for a time considerable confusion in the administration. Automatically every official in the State had lost his job, until re-appointed by the successor. Furthermore, as all the money in all the Treasuries in all the Kingdom was the personal property of the Maharaja it was all withdrawn (if there were time), so there was no money left to carry on the administration for a few months until some more revenue accumulated.

All male members of the Rana family, who were eligible to become Prime Minister in due course, were automatically Generals (those not eligible were only Colonels), and every department of the State—Law, Finance, Medical, Forestry, Post Office, etc., etc.—was under the charge of a General. The Nepalese Army had no lack of officers; a supreme Commander-in-Chief, a Commander-in-Chief, two or three Commanding Generals, a number of ordinary Generals, and many Colonels. On the other hand, it had no wheeled vehicles of any sort, and the artillery consisted of muzzle-loading black powder cannon, which made a grand noise and smoke at the numerous ceremonial parades. There was also no lack of wonderful uniforms and jewelled head-dresses for the senior officers, which made a splendid display at the durbars. I should, perhaps, explain that the Army was kept for three principal objects (i) to repel invasion on the mountainous frontiers, (ii) to keep internal peace and security, (iii) to make an impressive display at parades and festivals. The first of these did not arise, and the Army carried out the other two objectives most efficiently.

One of the features of life in Nepal, which impressed us very much, was the lack of opportunity for recreation and amusement for the general public. For example, there were no football, hockey or sports grounds, no race-course, no tennis courts, no theatre or cinema, no concert or dance halls, no public houses, no boxing or wrestling tourna-ments—literally nothing that one takes for granted in Europe or in India. Broadcasting sets were forbidden (except in the palaces) and there were no newspapers or journals, consequently there were no reporters, journalism or advertising. The general public had no way of hearing what was happening in the outside world, except rumour. This was all part of the general policy of no publicity and extreme secrecy.

By contrast, the telephone was so arranged to give the widest possible publicity. A telephone line (in lieu of a telegraph) connected Kathmandu with India and some provincial headquarters. There was no telephone exchange, but every station (there were about 14 of them) was connected with every other station, and a conversation between any two was automatically heard by all. Consequently not more than one conversation could be carried on at a time over the whole system. I remember once waiting an hour to telephone to Evelyn about the arrival of some Burma stamps that Bill had sent, they were overprinted with peacocks in various colours by the Japanese. A long telegram was coming in about the purchase of a number of dogs in Calcutta, and the two Nepali telephone operators had not the least idea how to pronounce or spell the names—Dachshund, Sealyham, and the like—and the operator at my end appealed to me for assistance. When my message finally went through it created a sensation all over Nepal, and was (of course) reported to the highest authorities. The message was, "A lot of peacocks have arrived, 10 blue, 20 black, 4 red and 2 double"!

Reverting to the subject of public amusements to make up for the lack of what are commonplace in other countries, Nepal has some very peculiar ones of its own, usually connected directly or indirectly with religious festivals. There is, for instance, the festival of Diwali, commemorating the Goddess of Luck. Gambling in Nepal is very strictly prohibited, except at this festival (and one or two other days of general rejoicing during the year, e.g. the Maharaja's birthday). At the firing of a gun a perfect orgy of gambling commences and continues for two days and two nights without a stop. The whole male population takes a hand, from greybeards to toddling boys. Every palace and house and bazaar shop has its gambling party, other parties spill over into the streets, which are blocked to traffic for the duration. There are various gambling games, but the most popular is played with 16 cowrie shells, which are round on one side and split on the other.

The "board," which as often as not is marked on the road, like children's hopscotch in Irish towns today, consists of four squares each square with four numbers; 1, 5, 9, 13 in one, 2, 6 10, 14 in the next, and so on, and a gambler sits at each square. The "dealer" shakes the 16 cowries in his hand like dice and throws them out. Suppose 9 cowries come to rest with the split side up, then the player at the square showing 9 gathers in all the stakes and becomes the "dealer" for the next throw. A simple game of chance requiring no skill, which we found very boring after half an hour, when we occasionally took a hand. But not so the Nepalese. It was an astonishing sight to go round the streets of Kathmandu at night during Diwali. At that festival, every building, from great palace to tiny hovel, every window, every balcony, every nook and cranny, is lit up with tiny oil lamps. In the light of thousands of these little flickering lamps, crowds fill the streets, congregating round the innumerable "gambling tables" in the roadways or in the shops, watching the players win and lose, starting new tables, or filling a vacancy as some unfortunate retires having lost his all. Children with tense faces stake their farthings, the poorer members of the population risk rupees or smaller silver coins, up at the palaces gambling is done with counters and enormous sums change hands. The settlement of these huge sums used to be quite a problem when there was no bank or banking system in Nepal, no payment by cheques, no local paper money. Settlement of debts had to be mostly in silver rupees, carried through the streets of Kathmandu. But by the time we went to Nepal, this had become rather rare, as a bank had been opened the previous year. Twenty years earlier stakes were not confined to coin or counters, but slaves, and even wives, were sometimes staked.

Another astonishing Hindu festival, to us at least, was Dashera. For a week or more before this festival was due, strings of animals would be met on all the roads leading to Kathmandu from surrounding districts, with baskets of poultry, sheep, goats, small buffaloes (but, of course, never cows, bulls or their progeny), for sale to the inhabitants of the town, and more particularly to the regiments and regimental officers, each of whom had to present two or three or more animals (according to his rank) to his regiment for the celebrations of the coming festival.

With the day of the festival there comes an orgy of sacrifice and slaughter without parallel in our experience. A rough estimate of 50,000 animals killed is probably well below the mark. And the bulk of this is not done in slaughter-houses or back-yards, but in the main streets and squares in the town, which are soon swimming in blood, providing a stinking and bloody spectacle for the populace. The chief excitement is connected with the regiments. Here the animals have to be completely decapitated *at one stroke* with a kukri, the famous curved sword of the Gurkha battalions. In the case of a sheep or goat this is easy, but when it comes to a young buffalo with a neck a foot or more across, and a thick spinal column, it is not so easy. If the striker succeeds, the feat is acclaimed with shouts of applause, but woe to him if he fails for then he and his clothes are immediately drenched with blood by the spectators, while someone else finishes the job of decapitation. By nightfall, in the light of lamps and flaring torches, great piles of beheaded bodies are seen flung to one side or corner of the main square, awaiting removal by the troops for a gargantuan meal. But the total supply of meat provided at this festival is far greater than can be eaten immediately, and for weeks afterwards many houses and balconies are festooned with long strips of meat drying in the open air and sun. Curiosity took us once to see the show, and once was enough. Thereafter we kept out of the town during Dashera.

There is another spectacle which takes place about the same time, a Nepali version of a bull fight. This is another astonishing sight, which is run by the Newars, the original inhabitants of the valley of Nepal before the Gurkha invasion.

The fight takes place at night in one of the city squares, which is paved with large flat slabs of rock, and surrounded with houses and shops whose windows and balconies are made of elaborately carved woodwork. They have more or less open verandahs raised a few feet above the level of the square which, on a bull-fight night, are crowded with spectators. But there are far more spectators than can be accommodated in them; the bulk of the people—only men and boys, no women—squat around the edge of the "bull-ring" itself, completely unprotected from the charges of the bulls except by their own quickness and agility in avoiding them.

The first time we were taken to a bull-fight the proceedings had already started. There was a young bull buffalo in the ring; he was being teased by three grotesquely dressed Newars; two with lances and spears, and one with a rather long straight and (to judge by results) not frightfully sharp sword. To start with the bull showed no animosity or resentment at the three figures dancing around him; it took a good quarter of an hour of pricks from the lances before he began to get annoyed. Then he began to charge, and the fun began.

The swordsman gave us the first thrill. He had fortified himself for the fight with country spirit but unfortunately to excess, and disgraced himself by falling down drunk when he turned to run; the bull prodded the prostrate body gently with his horns until driven off. The proceedings were then delayed a further 10 minutes while another swordsman was brought to take his place.

The new swordsman distinguished himself by giving the bull a hefty swipe on the top of the neck, which made an ugly gash, and so surprised the animal that he charged the side of the square near where we were sitting, leaped on to a verandah already crowded to suffocation with spectators, and dashed on into an equally crowded room! It was no joke for the terrified and unfortunate occupants but screamingly funny for everyone else. The majority bolted through the windows yelling murder, while a few of the more agile scrambled up on to the rafters and sat there out of the bull's reach.

Then followed another long hiatus while they tried to drive the beast back into the arena, but without success, until a cow buffalo was produced which enticed him out. So far the proceedings had on the whole been very funny, but now the Master of Ceremonies apparently thought that there had been enough fooling about, and three Newars appeared in the ring. For the next half hour or more, these swordsmen kept hacking away at the neck of the galloping animal, gradually enlarging the original slash, until the unfortunate creature sank down from loss of blood and exhaustion and was finally finished off with some more neck-hacking. Then the three Newars scooped some blood and meat in their hands and, dancing up before the Master of Ceremonies, proceeded to drink and eat the warm raw mess. This about finished me, and we hastily departed before the next bull buffalo was brought into the arena. The whole affair had been revolting, and I wonder what (*a*) a Spaniard, (*b*) a Blue Cross enthusiast, would have thought of it.

All Newar festivals, however, are not orgies of blood and massacre. There is a quaint festival which lasts four days, and on each day one variety of animal is venerated and petted. The first day it is the cow. Cows, of course, are sacred animals which are venerated and worshipped all the year round. But on this particular day they are also actually fed, an agreeable contrast to the other 364 days. Their bodies are painted with numerous blue spots about the size of small saucers, and as they wander about the streets their tails and rumps are affectionately stroked by passers-by.

The next day it is the turn of the dogs. Now dogs in Nepal—as elsewhere in the East—are not pampered Pekinese or anything like that, but usually half-starved mangy pie-dogs, often bald with ringworm or itch, for whom the kindest gift one used to imagine would be a lethal chamber. On this one day, however, dogs are fed and also petted. The third day it is the turn of the poultry, and the fourth day of the crows. Why the latter were chosen for veneration we never discovered.

One of the most striking and colourful of religious festivals in Nepal is in honour of Machhendranath, Nepal's patron saint. The story goes that untold centuries ago, in the golden age of Nepal, there lived a great saint called Machhendranath. One day he disappeared, but left behind him two things, i.e. one of his shirts, and a prophecy or promise that one day he would return to Nepal to claim his shirt. If the people had carefully preserved it, he would then come and live in Nepal again and, with his blessing and miraculous power, health, wealth, and prosperity—in fact a second golden age—would be bestowed on the people.

So every year on the appointed date a great ceremony is held of presenting the shirt to the people, so that if the holy saint Machhendranath has returned to Nepal during the year, he may come and claim it and thus usher in another glorious golden age. But the ceremony requires a great deal of preliminary preparation. The shirt is always displayed from a very special carriage or movable tower—I don't really know what to call it. It is a solid and immensely heavy wooden construction towering up 40 or 50 feet, resting on a platform, which is mounted on four enormous wooden wheels about 6 feet in diameter and a foot or more thick. The shafts, one sticking out in front and one behind, are enormous pieces of timber chiselled out of whole pine trees. I cannot guess how many tons the whole contraption weighs.

The ceremony is held on a *maidan* (anglice, flat piece of land like a football ground) near a particular temple and, incidentally, near the local zoo. But the fearsome chariot is kept in another part of the valley, several miles away, and has to be brought to the temple site, which involves much hard work and a major operation lasting a full month. It is quite a sight to see the great juggernaut crawling along inch by inch, tugged and pushed and pulled by a few hundred yelling Newars along the undulating and narrow road. Usually the Nepalese Army is mobilized to give a helping hand. Branches of trees have to be lopped to make room for the tower, and in places on the route the high tension cables of Kathmandu's electric supply have to be removed, leaving Kathmandu without current for a few hours.

After a month of strenuous effort the chariot arrives at the site of the ceremony. On the appointed day a public holiday is proclaimed. The Maharaja, the Diplomatic Corps, and all the Nobility of Nepal arrive in cars; the Nepalese Army is there to form a Guard of Honour and a hollow square, and the ceremony starts. His Highness the Maharaja mounts the platform, and solemnly holds up the Saint's shirt to the view of the public at each of the four corners, while a priest or someone calls a prayer to the Saint to come down and claim it if he is present.

The shirt itself, a dirty dark thing that might fit a child of six, always struck me as an amazing incredible anticlimax, following on the month of toil, the pomp and splendour of the parade, and especially in contrast to the gigantic car from which it is exhibited. It suggested also that the famous Saint must have been a very diminutive dwarf. During the centuries no one has yet come forward to claim it. One condition, to be fulfilled by any claimant, is that he should immediately perform some striking and supernatural miracle. This condition, combined with the tiny size of the shirt, has evidently been sufficient to choke off any impostors.

When no claimant comes forward the ceremony is completed, the shirt returned to safe custody of the temple for another year, and the juggernaut laboriously dragged back to its permanent home.

But these and other festivals, some Hindu and some peculiar to Nepal, still leave long dull blanks in the calendar when the Nepalis can find little to amuse them. There is, however, one form of pleasure or amusement which can be enjoyed the world over, which costs nothing, and requires no paraphernalia or organization, merely a man and a woman together. Here I must digress for a moment, and emphasize that we cannot judge Eastern standards and morals by our own standards. We do things, as a matter of course, which shock Hindus far more than anything they do would shock us. Eating beef, for example. In Nepal, of course, this was so absolutely prohibited that in seven years' residence we never even opened a bottle of Bovril! The Eastern outlook on sex relations is very different to ours. Prostitution, for example, is an honourable profession, and amongst Nepalis at least, it is a matter of religious belief that a man, who has 125 *different* women in this life, is sure of a very high place in the next!

There was a prelude to many a sylvan idyll which seemed a universal custom in the wooded mountains around Kathmandu, and in the hill tracts generally. When we were passing through these hill forests, either on tour or on a picnic, very frequently we heard a striking and characteristic duet ringing out across the open spaces from one ridge or slope to another, a man's voice answering a woman's musical notes in alternative verses. The tune consisted of the characteristic quavers of Eastern music, but each verse ended in a high-pitched and very long drawn-out note, quite unlike any other song. Having heard it a number of times, one day Evelyn asked one of our orderlies what the song was about and whether he could sing it. He admitted, rather bashfully, that he knew it quite well but flatly refused to sing it then, probably because I was present.

Later, he gave Evelyn further information, and explained the meaning of the song and its implications. "Somewhere a voice is calling, calling for me" is a possible analogy. A gay young spark from some hill village, out in the forest to collect fire-wood, or fungi, or something, starts off singing that he is a very pleasant fellow, but is all alone and lonely and would like a companion. If he is in luck, presently a girl's voice will take up the refrain, from half a mile away, and in the second verse explain that she also has attractions, and would be willing to be his companion for a while, but what inducements can he offer. Then the duet follows another and better analogy, the old English song, "Madam will you walk, Madam will you talk?" After he has offered her the Nepali equivalents of the keys of heaven, a gown of silk, a ring of gold, and the rest, with each verse the two singers gradually approach each other, and finally as they meet and he offers her the keys of his heart, she accepts his advances and the song gives way to a blissful silence.

In conclusion, I must emphasize that the contents of this chapter apply to an epoch that is gone, and many things are different in Nepal to-day.

# CHAPTER FIFTEEN

## *Crime Detection in Nepal*

IN Nepal, when all usual methods of crime detection fail, one invokes the help of the occult! We ourselves experienced an interesting and curious example of this.

Evelyn usually kept our spare cash for household expenses locked up in his office-box in the office-room, a practice I had often complained was unsafe, for the box could be forced open without great difficulty. Evelyn, however, pooh-poohed my fears and refused to keep the money locked up in our bed-room. Immediately after Evelyn had drawn his pay there was often quite an amount of cash in hand, Rs.500/- or more in currency notes and coin.

One afternoon we went out to play golf as we usually did two or three times a week; we left the box intact with Rs.480/- (£36) in currency notes and Rs.100/- in Nepali coin. There was no occasion to examine it that evening, but next morning my forebodings had come true, the lock of the office-box had been forced the currency notes all removed, and the silver all left. We immediately sent for the police. It was undoubtedly a robbery carried out by one of our servants between 5 p.m. and 9 a.m., as outside robbers had not broken in during the night, and could not have carried out the theft while the servants were about in the afternoon.

The Inspector of Police said he could probably discover the thief and recover the money if given a free hand. Knowing something about police methods in Nepal, we asked what exactly a "free hand" would involve. It was explained that the police would arrest half a dozen of our servants on suspicion, keep them in jail for two or three weeks if necessary, and apply the third degree until the culprit confessed. Apart from the inconvenience of having no servants for weeks, this was more than we were prepared to do, so we thanked the police for their kind assistance and said we would let them know later.

We then began to hear of remarkable cases where past thefts in Nepal had been discovered in miraculous ways by other means. There were apparently two or three *Hakims* or soothsayers who could see the past and explain exactly how and when and by whom the theft had been committed, and where the money now was. So we agreed to try this (to us) new method of crime detection.

The first *Hakim* to appear on the scene was quite normal. He asked for one rupee and a plate of rice and, being provided with these, started his antics. He threw grains of rice into the place, danced around a bit saying prayers and *mantras*, studied the rice grains carefully for some minutes, and then came out with the following. The robbery had been carried out at 7 o'clock in the morning by two of our Kesai servants, whom he described clearly, even to their clothes and features; they had an outside accomplice sitting on the wall of our garden to whom they immediately made over the money. By his occult powers and *mantras* he would put a spell on them, so that all three would meet at our gate in an hour's time, looking agitated and bereft of speech. It all sounded rather improbable, especially the third thief sitting conspicuously on a high wall in the morning sun. However, we waited an hour, by which time nothing had happened, and the *Hakim* had faded away and was no more seen. An obvious charlatan!

Meanwhile a second *Hakim* had appeared, who had a great reputation, having successfully recovered Rs.2,000/-

from a thief in the Legation a few months back. This man was peculiar in appearance. He had an enormous protruding lower lip that stuck out and hung over his chin for a couple of inches, a horrid sight. Also a peculiar right eye, with a whitish V sign—in appearance like a faint cataract—stretching from the pupil of the eye upwards. This man wanted Rs.2 and some rice, which were provided. His actions were not at all spectacular. Sitting in our verandah he burnt a twig over the plate of rice, muttering some prayers to himself. After a minute or two, turning towards the light, he said that anyone with good eyesight could see the thief carrying out the robbery by looking carefully into the white V mark in his eye. So Evelyn, taking off his shoes, squatted down, and stared hard at the man's eye, followed by one of his clerks and then another, but none of them could see anything.

The *Hakim* then said it would work better if a child or a woman looked into his eye. There happened to be a woman cutting grass in the garden so she was called up, looking timid and frightened, to see what she could do. Presently she said she could see a man's figure but could not describe it. Pressed to be a bit more explicit she said he was wearing a white vest without sleeves. This pointed to our Bengali cook.

The *Hakim* then said that if his wife looked into his eye she would explain everything that had happened clearly. So Evelyn's Assistant (a Nepali official) went off with the man to his home and came back an hour later, saying the wife had clearly described and implicated the same two Kesai servants as before, describing them accurately, where their homes were, and how they were now quarrelling over the division of the money. However, when accused of the theft these two men denied all knowledge of it, and even the usual custom, of giving them 24 hours to put the money back on the quiet with no further questions asked, failed.

Moreover Kesai servants would have taken the Nepali coins rather than Indian currency notes and thus avoid visits to money changers. This *Hakim* appeared to be another charlatan or confidence-trick merchant, who had picked up some information in our compound and somehow passed it on to his wife.

By this time a third *Hakim* had appeared. We were getting a bit weary of doling out rupees to frauds and stipulated that if he successfully recovered all the lost money he would get a substantial reward, otherwise nothing. To this he agreed, which seemed to indicate considerable faith in his own powers. His method was the Nepali equivalent of a method well known in psychic circles—a child, under occult influences, gazing into an inkpool.

In this case, the inkpool was replaced by a smear of shiny black substance on the palm of a little girl about nine years old, and we witnessed the seance, which was really remarkable. First the man did some small *puja* ceremony with some rice, which seems to be an essential preliminary in Nepal. Then, sitting by the little girl, he rubbed some of the black shiny substance on the palm of her hand; his throat muscles worked strongly, but without speech, and he made passes with his hands. Next he prayed to the unseen powers to help in the investigation, the little girl repeating each sentence after him. After this the child stared hard at the black spot on her palm, held level with, and close to, her eyes, but she did not appear to be in a trance or under hypnotic control in any way.

The *Hakim* asked her to describe anything she saw. There was a long pause, and then she began to speak. She began by describing in minute and accurate detail the office-room and its furniture, also the office-box, which had been broken open, i.e. "A black box, blue inside, with a red leather cover." This made us sit up and take notice as it was quite impossible for either the man or the child to have

K

seen the office-room, or its furniture, or the box, or to have received a detailed description of them.

She then went on to say that she saw a man entering the room, break the lock of the box forcibly with some instrument, and take the notes. She said there was one large note and many small ones (there was, in fact, one Rs.100/- note), and the man went out of the room to his quarters where he put some of the notes in a box, and he gave the rest to someone—not one of our servants—who took the money away to the bazaar. Her description of the thief tallied with our Bengali cook! She described the box in which some of the money had been put, "A red and green metal box." Further questioned, she said the theft was done in the evening when it was beginning to get dark.

On this Evelyn and his Assistant went to the cook's quarters, where they found a steel box painted in red and green as described and in which, when opened, they found a few Rs.10/- notes, which the cook could not satisfactorily account for, but no Rs.100/- note.

We had our own suspicions about this man. He had been seen shortly after 5 p.m. in the drawing-room next the office-room, where he had no business to be. He had recently taken a bad Nepali woman as wife, which had cost him a pretty penny, and he had been seen speaking to one of her relations that same evening in our drive. All this fitted in very well with what the little girl had described as seeing in the blackness of her hand. Even then, however, we could not hand him over to the police, and preferred to do without the money rather than to try and retrieve it by this means. So instead we dismissed him. He seemed very relieved and streaked out of Nepal while the going was good. In many ways he was a great loss for he was an excellent cook.

This case might not have obtained a conviction in a court of law, but we believe that the ignorant little Nepali girl, in some occult way did, in fact, describe accurately what had happened. Anyway she certainly described the office-room, the office-box and the cook's box with complete accuracy, without ever seeing them or having them described to her.

# CHAPTER SIXTEEN

## *A Maharaja's Shoot*

Fʀoᴍ the days of the Mogul Emperors, and earlier still, tiger hunting has been a favourite sport of the rulers of India, and nowhere more so than in Nepal, with the unparalled opportunities that wild jungle country provides.

Jung Bahadur, that amazing and almost mythical character who started as a catcher of wild elephants and ended as the Prime Minister and Supreme Ruler, the Founder of the Rana dynasty which ruled Nepal for 100 years, was able to indulge in his passion for big game hunting, and in 30 years is said to have killed 550 tigers! Contemporary paintings of tiger hunting in the Nepal Terai 100 years ago give a vivid impression of the thrills of big game hunting by comparatively primitive means and methods in those early days. Sometimes the tiger was brought to bay by a posse of elephants, occasionally he was attacked at close quarters on foot with sword and spear. Wherever Jung Bahadur camped, enquiries were made from the local villagers regarding recent kills or where tigers had been seen or heard, and on such uncertain information an area was beaten by elephants in the hope that the tiger might be inside. In those days the number of tame elephants in Nepal was enormous, and Jung Bahadur frequently had as many as 700 for his *shikar*. But the uncertain methods of locating tigers did not at first produce very good results. Later Jung Bahadur created a special service of 120 *shikaris*, whose duty it was to find fresh tiger tracks and other signs, to tie up baits (goats at first and later young buffalo calves), and quickly send in news of any kills. It was Jung Bahadur, who first evolved and developed the "Ring" method, which was gradually elaborated and improved by later Maharajas into the supremely efficient system finally employed.

Before attempting to describe a Maharaja's shoot, it will help the reader to visualize the scene if a description is first given of the method almost invariably used in all big shoots in Nepal, the famous and unique "Ring." This method is used only in Nepal, where it has been brought to an art, the highest pitch of perfection, and a most deadly method of killing all big game. There is in fact no other country in the world where the necessary factors for the "Ring" shoot exists, the enormous stud of *shikar* elephants, the trained experience and skill of their *mahawats* and the *shikaris*, the tremendous stretches of Terai forests, and the wonderful stock of tiger and rhino.

The natural home of tiger is the forest-clad foothills of of the Churia (Siwalik) range of the Himalayas, with the enclosed duns and valleys, and the adjoining forests of the flatter Terai. This great belt of tiger country stretches the whole length of Nepal, a distance of nearly 550 miles on the map, and for more than half the year it is deadly to man owing to the malignant Terai malaria. But from December to March it is a perfect paradise, with a glorious climate, wonderful scenery, and always to the north the incredible panorama of the eternal snows towering into the sky.

In this superb setting occur the big Nepal shoots to which many distinguished guests have been invited including King George V. A wonderful organization is employed to ensure success. For weeks before the shoot commences, rough but serviceable motor roads and temporary bridges are constructed radiating out from the various jungle camps. All the jungle paths and streams and sandy river beds are examined to see where the tigers are, for in such places they leave their footmarks. A day or two before the shoot starts, young buffalo calves are tied up as bait, in scores or even hundreds, on every likely route a tiger may take. (The cow, being venerated, its progeny cannot be used for tiger bait.)

There are seven or eight groups of regularly appointed *shikaris*, each consisting of an officer (*subedar*), 10 or 12 subordinates, and two mounted soldiers for taking messages. Every group of *shikaris* has 10 to 15 buffalo calves (*padahs*) for tying up at suitable places. They live in temporary sheds in the jungle, primitive huts of wooden poles, leaves and jungle grasses fastened with strands of creepers, which they quickly erect with their kukris from the abundant material all around. Between them the various groups cover the whole tract of forest for miles around the central camp.

At dawn the *shikaris* go out and examine the *padahs*, tied out the previous evening. If, or when, one has been killed, they carefully examine pugmarks (footprints) to see if it is a big tiger or small, or one or several. They examine the drag and the direction taken. They then quietly proceed on foot and make a large circle of a quarter to a half mile diameter, demarcating the circumference with chipped stems and grass knots as they go, and are very careful to see that the drag has not gone beyond the circle. If it has, they make another one, as they must have the circle enclosing the end of the drag. This is called "cutting the circle" by the *shikaris*, and the final circle makes the future "Ring."

Meanwhile, as soon as it is seen that a *padah* has been killed and dragged, a special messenger mounts his horse, and gallops off to bring the news. Sometimes motor cars are parked at central spots to accelerate the delivery of the message, and sometimes even a telephone line has been prepared and operators engaged to flash news to the camp.

Within a very short time the news has reached the camp from all directions whether and where there are kills, and the day's plan of campaign is discussed and settled. Immediately a great string of 200 or 300 elephants moves off in single file to the first kill, a few with howdahs, the majority with pads. The shooting party follows at leisure in cars as far as possible, and then on pad elephants.

The tiger or tigers have been approximately located by the *shikaris* from the direction of the drag, the nature of the cover for lying up, and the process of cutting the circle as already described. When the elephants arrive, they divide into two parties, which proceed very quietly in single file right and left along the line of the cut circle—and it is astonishing how quietly an elephant or line of elephants can move through the jungle. The rear elephants gradually drop out to take their stations at regular intervals, and finally the two leading elephants meet and the word is passed down both sides that the circuit is completed.

The shooting party mount the howdah elephants and the whole circle now moves inwards, crushing the grasses and shrubs, and the men on their backs shouting and whistling to drive the tiger towards the centre. The circumference of the circle of elephants gets smaller, until finally it is less than half a mile round, and the elephants get closer and closer until they are almost touching, and the tiger is surrounded by a solid wall of elephants. Then the order—stop the line—is shouted out and the ring is complete.

The stauncher elephants then move into the ring. Glimpses of one or more slinking forms are seen in the grass and undergrowth, when suddenly a tiger breaks cover and charges with a roar, to be met by shots from the rifle or shouts and missiles if he charges the ring. It is the moment of climax of a culminating excitement. Backwards and forwards he dashes striving to find an escape, to a pandemonium of men shouting and elephants trumpeting, grumbling and gurgling, thumping on the ground and, occasionally, when directly charged turning tail and bolting in terror.

It is necessary to emphasize that a tiger is not normally a

dangerous animal and does not attack an elephant or a man, but once he feels cornered, he becomes a fighting mass of diabolical fury utterly fearless of man or elephant, whom he attacks in his mad rage without a moment's hesitation. He has been known to leap a height of 15 or 16 feet into a tall howdah, and more often than not a tiger will try to break through a ring by charging home on an elephant unless he is killed or crippled first by a well-directed shot.

It must also be realized that the Nepal Terai jungles with a fertile soil and rainfall of 100 inches are either gigantic grass growth, frequently the height of a howdah, or are a dense forest of trees, matted together with great climbers and a thick undergrowth of shrubs and shade-bearing plants in which, if an elephant bolts, it is almost inevitable that howdah and rider and *mahawat* and everything on the elephant's back will be swept with a crash to the ground by a thick branch or the loop of a tough climber. In either case it is extremely difficult to see a tiger at all until the area has been well trampled, by which time, naturally, the tiger or tigers are desperate and in a highly dangerous condition. "It is no sport for bad shots, hasty excitable people, or those with no stomach for danger. Even the most blasé hunter is likely to experience for a second or two a sudden spasm of fear when he first hears the blood-curdling roar of an infuriated tiger, and sees the great striped body launched in its charge, a thunder-bolt of death and anger in mid-air. It is one of the most terrific sights in the world."*

Imagine what it must be like when, as frequently happens in the rings in Nepal, not one, but four or five and, once or twice, six tigers have been trapped simultaneously in one ring! The danger and heart-bursting excitement may continue for hours, until a succession of well-placed shots finally brings the thrill and nerve-tension to an end.

That describes briefly a typical tiger shoot in the Nepal

* Wentworth Day's *King George V as a Sportsman.*

*Plate 7*    A Viceroy's shoot in chitawan, with elephants crossing the river Rapti on their way to form a "ring" The eternal snows in the distance.

forests by the famous "Ring" method. Personally I never thought that this was a very sporting way of shooting tigers as they did not seem to have much chance of escaping with their lives.

The whole marvellous organization is itself unrivalled; the elaborate arrangements for locating every tiger for miles around—by skilled parties of *shikaris*, the quick receipt of information, the great stud of well-trained elephants with their splendid and plucky Tharu *mahawats*, the methods to prevent the encircled tiger from breaking the ring and escaping, all this, with first-class shooting, make such a deadly combination that few tigers can escape. In fact, if repeated at too frequent intervals in any locality, there would be a considerable risk of tigers becoming exterminated in that locality. In Nepal, however, although the stock of tigers has no doubt been reduced appreciably (at the start their numbers were excessive, and they did much damage to village cattle), extermination was safeguarded by two factors. One was the expanse of broken hill forests, where the ring method cannot be used, which forms a natural sanctuary and breeding ground for tiger. The other was that with tiger country stretching along the foot of the hills for 550 miles, there was such a vast tract to visit that the Maharaja could have shoots with the ring method without frequent visits to any one locality.

A few concrete examples, selected from innumerable cases recorded in the official shooting diary of Maharaja Jodha Shumshere, will illustrate how the "Ring" works. One year in January, three guests had been invited, the British Minister in Nepal, a distinguished American naturalist, and a film operator. They had indeed a day to remember!

The ring was 8 miles from the camp and provided hours of excitement. This locality was characterized by very heavy grass taller than the elephants and undergrowth in which it was almost impossible to see the quarry. A tiger was first put up at which two shots were fired. The noise disturbed *four* more tigers, so there were five tigers in all enclosed (2 tigers, 2 tigresses and a large cub, i.e. two families). It was a nerve-racking business to tackle so many tigers in that tremendous grass in which they could lie unseen within a few feet of the elephants. They were moving about, growling and slinking unseen, without offering a shot to the marksmen. Suddenly pandemonium broke out at one section of the line, elephants trumpeting, fidgeting and curling up their trunks, with the usual accompaniment of shouts and yells, clearly indicating that one or more tigers were trying to escape that way. At last after further beating, a tiger came out where the undergrowth had been trampled, and was killed.

The ring was beaten again, and a tiger leapt on to the rump of one of the beating elephants, and stayed on for several yards before dropping off. The American guest fired and killed it. Again the howdahs and beating elephants went through the heavy grass, and six shots were fired at intervals as one or another tiger showed itself for a moment. The next to fall was a tigress.

By this time the sun had set, but there were still two tigers in the ring, and the howdahs turned once more into the heavy grass. For a change, the next tiger charged the ring. A pad elephant, panic-stricken, whisked round and bolted, throwing off its *mahawat* and passenger to the ground. They were however unscathed by the fall, or by the tiger, and were quickly mounted on another elephant. This tiger broke through and escaped.

It was now 6.45 p.m. on a winter night, and the light had completely gone. But still there was another tiger in the ring, a tigress as it happened, and by now a fury incarnate. It was a weird amazing scene, a nocturne of the jungle, where nothing could be seen except the crowns of the scattered trees against the glimmer of stars. Then the hunt took on a different aspect, as resinous torches blazed out all round, and by their light the tigress was at last spotted and shot. Four tigers in one ring, the last killed by torchlight! Was ever *shikar* like this before?

Occasionally, however, the proceedings did not go according to plan, and the sportsmen in the ring found themselves in considerable danger, as happened in the following episode. A tiger and tigress were put up and wounded; both wounded animals retired into thick cover in the middle of the ring. Nothing could be seen of them in the undergrowth, but suddenly, from a range of 8 feet, the tiger leapt on to the Maharaja's elephant, Bhimgaj, catching hold high up on the trunk, and started savagely biting and clawing. The other elephants turned tail and commenced to bolt, but Bhimgaj vigorously counter-attacked, and tried to kill the tiger by crushing it on the ground. This meant that the elephant was almost standing on his head, and "the howdah was tilted downwards almost to the ground. There seemed to be no possibility of the men in the howdah keeping their position. If they fell out, they would inevitably fall into the jaws of death." (The second wounded tiger was circling around, near its mate.) In this critical situation, deafened by the mad roaring of the tigers and the trumpeting of the elephants, the Maharaja and his A.D.C. by some miracle successfully avoided being hurled out of the howdah. For minutes, which seemed like hours, this life and death struggle between elephant and tiger continued, while any attempt at shooting was out of the question. A superb painting of this dramatic moment by the photographer-artist, who was an eye-witness of it, hung for years in the great Durbar Hall in Kathmandu. Whether it is still there I do not know. Finally, the elephant drew back with its trunk severely mauled, and the tiger was finished off.

Tigers were not the only big game that was hunted in Nepal for the famous Chitawan sanctuary was the home of several hundred rhino, which were very strictly preserved. In this rhino preserve posts were stationed at various points, each post manned by five to seven guards. In all there were over 100 guards in Chitawan, whose main duty was to protect the rhino from poachers, and find out where they fed and wallowed. The fact that the rhino horn has a very high commercial value in India—a good horn is worth well over £100—makes it a valuable prize for the professional poacher, and the species was nearly exterminated in Assam by poachers until adequate steps were taken for its protection. (Rhino horn is supposed to be a powerful aphrodisiac, hence its fantastic value.) We were told that in years gone by, the penalty for unlawfully killing a rhino was 75 *hereditary* years imprisonment!

When hunting rhino, the "Ring" method frequently fails and for the following reason. Elephants, despite their great bulk and strength, are naturally timid animals, and even small animals like cats or porcupines in their vicinity make them nervous and restless. But of all things that elephants fear most, the rhino is *facile princeps*. Most elephants bolt at the mere sight of a rhino and very few are staunch. A rhino in a ring has only to charge the ring to break it in confusion and make his escape, and although rhino have been shot in rings, the more usual practice is to stalk them, or track them down with three or four of the staunchest elephants available.

Rhino shooting is sufficiently exciting of itself, but when wild bees take a part, they add painful variety and still more excitement. It may be mentioned in passing that there is nothing more dangerous in the Indian jungles and nothing more detestable, than to disturb a large swarm of the big venomous wild bees when engaged in trying to finish off a wounded tiger. They come down in their thousands and start stinging every living thing in sight; the elephants get wild and the tigers get wilder. Attempts to flee are futile, one might as well try to flee from a dive-bomber. However, the elephant and his driver very often do not appear to know this, and the possibility of one's elephant bolting through the forest adds further complications. In any case, whether the elephant flees or stays, it is quite certain that the *shikari* on its back will get stung, and may be badly stung, without the protection of a bee net—or a smoke screen.

This once occurred when a ring was being formed for a rhino hunt and, to quote from the official records: "The bees scattered about creating panic, furiously stinging every man in the ring. There was no escape from them, clouds of bees were everywhere and their ceaseless threatening hum in our ears. Everyone pulled off his coat and covered his face but none was left unstung." However, after a time the bees departed and when the ring was reformed, it seemed alive with rhino, 10 or 12 becoming visible! One was shot, and the blood libation ceremony had to be performed, but the presence of numerous live rhino still in the ring made this very difficult. Elephants, as previously mentioned, hate the proximity of rhino and they refused to approach them close. They were goaded on a few steps forward with difficulty and then they retreated to their original positions, and "for a whole hour the scene became one of rhinos and elephants moving forward and backward." A minuet of the pachyderms! Finally when the rhinos had retired in good order, "the dead rhino's entrails were laid aside, giving the dead animal the appearance of a big canoe. The blood libation was then performed."

I must explain what the blood libation ceremony is; to Western ideas it is a most astounding ceremony. It is connected with the sacred Shradda ceremony of the Hindus, and it will be interesting to give a brief description. Every year the head of a Hindu family has to make this religious performance on the anniversary of his father's death, and again in some particular fortnight a similar ceremony in honour of all his departed ancestors. Part of the ceremony consists of pouring water out of a vessel. If the vessel used can be a hollowed rhino horn, the ceremony increases very greatly in value. If further, the libation can be rhino blood this again very greatly enhances the importance of the ceremony. This is called the *Khadga-rudhir Tarpan* ceremony. Finally, if the offer of the rhino blood from a rhino horn can be made from inside the body of the rhino, it is of such high merit that the ancestors are freed from re-incarnations in their journey to Nirvana. Hence when a rhino is killed, the great mass of bowels and entrails are removed, leaving a vast cavity into which the man crawls to make the blood libation.

Wild elephants do not normally figure as the hunted in a Maharaja's shoot, but they sometimes create considerable diversion. A large herd of tame female elephants is a great attraction to a solitary wild tusker when they invade his domain, and he is liable to hang about a shooting camp.

The Maharaja had arranged a shoot for a Viceroy and the camp was being prepared. News was received that a tusker was in the forest to the east of the camps, and while a party of female elephants was reconnoitring along a broad stream, he suddenly appeared from the dense tree forest, and came towards the small female elephants who rapidly retired. Large reinforcements of tame elephants including some of the big fighting tuskers, were collected and advanced on the wild one who, as the official record puts it, "did not care a fig." More of the fighting elephants arrived and stood around the wild one, but were unwilling to attack. However, with the increased numbers and the yelling of the *mahawats*, the wild one turned round and ran away, to be followed hell-for-leather by the whole pack. That night the big tusker walked through the Nepalese camp, nearly upsetting the tent of one of the Generals, and next morning he was in evidence again. To quote the official diary: "The band played at 10.15 a.m. before the Viceroy's camp. Sixty of them, while returning to their encampment, met the wild elephant, and were paralysed in nervous fear. One fell upon the other, and the whole party became a solid entangled mass. However, when a party of orderlies arrived, they started up on their legs and departed to their lodgings."

Some days later, after the Viceroy and his party had left, the wild tusker, an animal of phenomenal size, was seen in a stream near the camp. The Maharaja seized the opportunity to try a new form of sport, resulting in one of the most amazing incidents that has ever been reported. He gave instructions that, if possible, the wild elephant should be brought into the stream bed below a high bluff, 50 feet high, from where an elephant fight could be watched in safety.

At 3.31 p.m. the wild elephant was seen approaching the stream, and the Maharaja, the senior Maharani with her attendants, the Generals and Staff, went and sat down on benches and seats on top of the bluff, below which it was hoped to stage the elephant fight. But the wild elephant would not come out into the stream bed of his own accord, and showed an indication of going back into the forest. So a number of female elephants went across to entice him out, and he rose to the occasion and followed them into the open.

The big fighting tuskers Bikram Prasad and Bahadur Prasad were then brought out to attack him, but refused to advance and, in fact, the latter, despite his name (Bahadur means brave) turned tail and ran away. But a comparatively small *makna* (a tuskless male) called Ram Prasad, with his *mahawat* and *pachwa* (the man who stands behind), with incredible pluck on the part of man and beast alike crashed forward, and began to fight. It must be realized that the wild elephant was of huge size and weight, and had powerful sharp-pointed tusks. What a wonderful setting for a primeval titanic fight, with the Maharaja, the ladies and high officials of the court looking down on the jungle stream bed, and the dense high forest behind, watching a scene that civilized men have seldom seen—the wild elephant fighting in his jungle haunts for his life and freedom! To quote from the diary:

The tussle was a very thrilling one, and although his trunk was wounded by the tusk of the wild elephant, Ram Prasad knocked him about and the *mahawat* wounded him with his lance. No other elephant would go forward to help against the wild one. For four or five minutes the fight continued and the spectacle was most exciting and dramatic. Then our elephants made an encircling movement round the wild elephant at close quarters, who turned and bolted away along the stream banks, and Ram Prasad pursued his rival, striking him with his trunk, pulling his tail, and trying to entangle his back legs, while the *mahawat* too made thrusts with his lance in an admirable manner, and the whole pack of tame elephants followed closely behind. It was a very fine sight to see the wild one being pursued by the domestics like a hawk is sometimes pursued by a flock of crows.

Then a surprising reverse took place, as the wild elephant suddenly turned back and charged his rival Ram Prasad violently from a vantage ground which placed the smaller elephant at a disadvantage. Ram Prasad retired, but the wild elephant turned him over and began to gore the prostrate body with his tusks at various points, sometimes on the head, sometimes on the limbs. For some time he placed his feet upon the body and tried to crush it with his mighty weight. The *pachwa* jumped off Ram Prasad's back at the first onset, but the *mahawat* was seen going down with the falling *makna*, and all the beholders cried out in pity for the poor *mahawat*, thinking it was all over with him. But God's will is wonderful, and the impossible sometimes turns out to be possible. Jaghan Dhari, the *mahawat*, was in imminent danger of being crushed by the weight of his own elephant, but in some miraculous way he was jerked off and fell behind the hind legs of the wild elephant, and crawled away into safety.

The wild elephant was about to kill Ram Prasad, when a party went forward and resorted to blank firing. This did not drive off the infuriated elephant, but a bullet in the leg at last made it fly into the jungle.

Ram Prasad was prostrate, and a large number of men were employed in giving him some relief when the Maharaja went down to inspect the daring fighter, who had earned for himself immortal renown by his unexampled bravery. Ram Prasad could not be moved at that time, and orders were given that a number of men should keep guard over him with guns and torches during the night, as a precaution against the almost certain return of the wild one to the scene of the fight.

Doctors were engaged in dressing the wounds, which were terrible, and men with explosives, crackers and guns were ready against accidents, when the wild elephant returned again in the night, and although it was scared away for a time by the report of guns, it returned again. The prostrate Ram Prasad got its wind and, with superb courage, staggered to his feet and advanced towards the jungle as if he wanted to have another bout. But a dozen female elephants were able to obstruct him, and he was taken to a more comfortable place about 300 yards away. The trunk, legs, neck, and thigh were injured very severely, he could not raise his trunk, which was much swollen.

This plucky fighting elephant died a few days later from his wounds. His equally heroic *mahawat* escaped unhurt.

Two days later, on 15th December, the wild tusker turned up again in the night and created some trouble, so orders were given to try and capture him! A party of 10 or 15 female elephants, 8 or 10 tuskers, and 3 or 4 men with guns, accordingly set out to tackle the wild elephant. One is lost in admiration of the pluck of these Nepalese, who, having seen for themselves two days before what this elephant could do when roused, set out again to try and capture him alive! The elephant was soon found, and this time Bahadur Prasad lived up to his name and reputation, and, assisted by other tuskers, soon put the wild tusker to flight. For mile after mile the great beasts went crashing through the forests, smashing down saplings and shrubbery, tearing down lianes and creepers. Whenever the wild

L

elephant tried to turn or rest, Bahadur Prasad and Jaya Prasad, urged on by their *mahawats*, at once attacked with trunk and tusks. After three and a half hours, the wild elephant was run to a standstill. Bahadur Prasad and Bikram Prasad, the two biggest tame tuskers, closed in, one on either flank, and pressed him firmly onward towards the bed of a nearby stream with flowing water. Here the elephants began to drink thirstily, and while the wild tusker was so engaged and prevented by side pressure from turning round, the other *mahawats* came up behind and quickly fastened nooses and strong ropes, tying the back legs together, and the great beast was captured! One admires the combination of pluck and skill of the Nepalese which brought this exciting *shikar* to a successful conclusion.

These true stories are no longer of our day and age, but belong to an epoch and régime that passed away a decade ago. The characteristics of present-day Nepal, such as air services, hotels, press correspondents, tourists, and mountaineers—if we can judge by the numerous books recently published—were still very strictly prohibited at that time. There is no Maharaja now with unlimited powers and resources to organize such shoots, and we were fortunate to live in Nepal while such spectacular shoots were still in fashion, which enables me to describe them.

# CHAPTER SEVENTEEN

## *Journey to Burma*

BEFORE leaving Nepal and the East for ever I planned a
visit to Burma to see Bill, who was in the Forest Service
working at Mandalay. The war was over, but travelling
was still difficult and Burma was in a very unsettled state.
Evelyn was against the journey, in fact, everyone I met
advised me not to attempt it. However, Bill said that he
considered it would be safe for me to go so long as I left
again at the end of January. He fixed that date because
General Aung San headed a mission in January to the
British Government, to demand independence within a
year. This was granted by Attlee; if it had been refused
Aung San would have organized a country-wide rising
against the British on his return from London, and we
should have had to fight another Burmese war.

I journeyed by train to Calcutta, where I stayed with Bill
and Joyce Hands in their enormous house in Camac Street;
Bill was Presidency Commissioner. At that time Hindus
and Mahommedans were murdering each other in the
streets—sometimes there were pitched battles—thousands
of people were butchered.

Had I not been staying with the Hands I should have been
very nervous. I remember one night when tanks were
patrolling the streets, and we could plainly hear the roar of
an angry mob from a nearby bazaar. It was the most
terrifying sound I had ever heard and I could not sleep. As
I lay awake I thought of the mere handful of Europeans in
Calcutta compared to the hundreds of thousands of Indians.

It was men like Bill Hands who saved us from a truly terrible fate; I was thankful to be under his roof. Actually, just at that time Indians were fighting each other and not the British as was their usual custom. At any moment, however, they might turn against the Europeans.

The man in the travel agency was not at all helpful, and I could see he was not going to give me a berth for weeks. I applied for, and obtained, an interview with the Controller of Passages who asked me why I wanted to go to Burma; I replied that I wanted to see my son, who had been a Chindit in the war. This, apparently, was an excellent reason, the Controller said too much could not be done for these fine men. He gave me a No. 1 Permit, which forced the hand of the unwilling clerk in the travel agency; he was obliged to give me a berth on the next boat. He so arranged it, however, that I had very poor accommodation. The ship was crowded. I shared a two-berth (converted to a four-berth) cabin with a woman and her three children, one a small baby. The voyage lasted for three days and three nights. As I was lucky to be on the ship at all, I felt I could not grumble.

Bill met me in Rangoon, and took me to the Chief Conservator's house where he was staying. At that time there were no hotels in Rangoon; the city had been devastated by both armies, and by bombing and looting; whole streets were in ruins. I was appalled to see the damage.

Next day we left by train for Mandalay. The train was made up of what had formerly been third-class carriages, with hard wooden seats. We shared our compartment with a European, his wife and their Burmese maid. By a stroke of luck, I had brought a lilo with me, which we found invaluable; we blew it up and sat in comfort. There was, of course, no restaurant car; Bill had brought some provisions, and we could buy fruit and eggs when we stopped at stations; the journey took 24 hours. When we were asleep that night, the Burmese maid lit a huge cheroot—the "whacking white cheroot" of Kipling's song—which soon filled the carriage with fumes of strong tobacco. I woke nearly choking and could see the glowing tip of the cheroot at which the maid puffed happily. She was not at all pleased when I asked her to put it out.

The bridges on the line were all Bailey bridges, the original ones having been wrecked. As we went along I saw many engines and wagons lying derelict by the way; the stations were all in ruins.

Mandalay had been practically razed to the ground. There was hardly one building left intact in this once fine city. The station had no roof, the famous palace of the Burmese Kings inside the Fort had been burned, the whole place was in ruins. There was, of course, no hotel which was awkward. Bill was living as a paying guest with some Europeans who, rather unwilling, agreed to take me in as well. The room I was given had a large shell hole through it, and the bath and sanitary arrangements did not work. For the first time in my life I had a bath from a bucket!

There were many Japanese in Mandalay technically called "surrendered personnel." I saw them wandering about quite freely; they were to my mind, far too well treated, when one thought of the inhuman and atrocious way in which they had treated our men. It was astonishing to see how many of them wore spectacles.

Bill had a 15-cwt. truck, also a station wagon, both supplied by Government for his work. Every night he had to chain the truck and the car to pillars in the verandah of the house, and put the batteries indoors to prevent theft. While I was in Mandalay, a Police Officer left his car on the road in Maymyo while he went to look at the golf course; he was still in sight of the car when it was stolen!

Bill had a fine launch on the Irrawaddy. He was in charge

of timber supplies in Upper Burma, and had to do a great
deal of travelling both by river and road. He arranged to
take me on his next voyage up the river, and I was thrilled
at the prospect.

We went on board one evening after dinner. The launch
had a nice cabin with a single berth; it was small, but there
was just room for Bill to sleep on the floor. The lilo again
came in very useful. We had with us Bill's trusted Kachin
orderly, called Samdu Mai, also his Burmese cook and a
crew of five. Bill scorned to take an armed guard, which
some officials were doing.

Next morning we were off at 7.30. It was a glorious day;
we sat on deck basking in the sun, which was not too hot.
At mid-day we stopped and landed to see the Mingun
Pagoda with its great bell, weighing about 70 tons, the
largest suspended bell in the world. The pagoda was
designed by a mad king early in the 19th century to be the
largest in the world; a model is kept in Mingun to show
what it would have looked like if it had ever been completed. The bottom was to be an enormous square plinth
about 200 feet in height to carry the pagoda proper, which
was to rise a further 300 feet. Work went on for over 30
years, but when the king died not even the plinth had been
completed, although it had been built to a height of over
150 feet. It remains to this day the largest pile of bricks in
the world, rent from top to bottom by earthquake shocks of
the past 100 years. It would be incorrect to say that it is
a monument to the folly of a mad king, because it is the
Buddhist belief that a mortal acquires merit by the building
of a pagoda, and naturally the greater the pagoda the greater
the merit. One of the most striking sights of a trip on the
Irrawaddy is the countless succession of white pagodas
along the ridges and hill-tops.

That night we tied up at Kyaukmyaung. The Burmese
boy cooked us a delicious curry, which I thought was much

better than an Indian one; we washed it down with coffee made in a Cona. We were off again at dawn, and had a wonderful day going up the third Defile past Shwe-U-Taung mountain, which is a game sanctuary, one of the last remaining haunts of rhinoceros in Burma. Bill pointed out many interesting birds and, being a great ornithologist, he was able to tell me all about them and their habits. I was surprised to see no crocodiles, but Bill told me that no one has ever seen a crocodile on the Irrawaddy.

One of the principal exports from Burma used to be (and, perhaps, still is) large timber logs of teak and other species. These huge logs are felled in the jungles, where there are no roads, dragged by well-trained elephants to the nearest floating creeks and in the Monsoon come out on the Irrawaddy where they are made up into rafts.

We met several rafts of logs floating downstream. These were rafts of what is known in Burma as "In-kanyin" and in the timber trade as Eng or Gurjun, members of the great family of *Dipterocarpaceae*, of which the *sal* tree of northern India is, perhaps, the most famous example. Mandalay used to have 17 sawmills, and an annual production of 100,000 tons of this timber most of which supplied the wants of Central Burma, but a little of the best quality was sold to England. Bill's job was to get this trade on its feet again, by financing the timber traders and sawmillers, placing contracts for sawn timber (urgently required by the army, railways, etc.), arranging for rafting ropes, and so on. The timber does not float, so elaborate rafts have to be constructed. They are made up in sections containing about 12 logs, with either a bundle of bamboos, or a log of very light timber, between every two logs of in-kanyin to give the requisite buoyancy. It is a trade that goes back to the time of the Burmese kings, and over the years the people of the upper Irrawaddy have acquired great skill in handling these heavy and unwieldy rafts, often containing 300-400 tons of logs, in the swift currents. The Scylla and Charybdis of this voyage are firstly the danger of stranding on a sand-bank when the river level is falling, and secondly of being caught in one of the three or four notorious whirlpools. If caught by Scylla, the raft becomes high and dry, the bamboos rapidly crack in the hot sun, and the salvage becomes a most expensive business (the whole raft has virtually to be remade); whereas if sucked into Charybdis, the raft goes round and round, banging against the bank on each circuit, until the canes, binding the raft, snap under the strain, and the raft becomes a total loss.

The rafts tie up every night, and the stopping of a 300-ton raft, travelling at 4 knots down the river, is an exciting performance, yet achieved by the simplest of apparatus. A very long length of 4½-inch circumference coir rope (soaked in hot oil at the time of manufacture, to make it float) is attached to the end of the raft; the other end is taken ashore in a canoe, the men paddling furiously, and several turns thrown round a pole (6 feet long and roughly sharpened at one end), which is held at an angle of about 20°. As the strain comes on the rope, the tension tends to force the pole deeper into the sand, so that it does not slip. If the strain on the rope becomes too great, so that there is danger of it snapping, the men holding it allow it to slip a few feet at a time; the raft swings towards the bank on an arc, and gradually comes to rest alongside the bank. It is when the rope breaks (as it sometimes does in inexperienced hands) that the fun really begins.

The whole voyage takes anything from a week to a month, depending on the state of the water and any mishaps that occur. The men build one or two small huts on the raft and live in them.

We spent the night at Tagaung, where one column of Wingate's Force had crossed the Irrawaddy. Next morning we woke to find ourselves in a thick fog which gradually

*Plate 8A*

*Plate 8B*

"Hathis piling teak" in the virgin forests of Burma, and dragging logs
to the nearest floating stream.

dispersed as the sun rose. It was very peaceful chugging up the river; the current was extremely strong, and our fast launch only made slow progress. Bill pointed out where General Fergusson's Column crossed the river from Tigyaing to Myadaung. Our thoughts went back to the war, and to the men who had endured so much in the places through which we were now passing.

We saw many wrecks of small steamers; I had started to count them at the beginning of our voyage but there were so many that I had to give up. Many of them had been sunk so that they should not fall into the hands of the Japanese; they were further examples of the universal war damage all over Burma, lying half submerged, sometimes only a funnel showing above the water. We tied up at Inywa, where we spent the night. We went for a walk on shore to a Burmese village; I was a little nervous that we might be captured by Communists, so Bill, to humour me, carried a gun. In the village we bought some ripe bananas, which were a nice dessert at supper. That night we felt the launch rocking violently in quite a severe earthquake.

From Inywa it was a three-hour run to Katha, where some work was waiting for Bill's attention. Katha is a small town, the headquarters of the local Forest Department, the Civil Authorities and the Police. We were met by Mr Mustill, the Divisional Forest Officer. He told us that the day before there had been trouble with the Communists in the town and, therefore, it would not be safe for us to remain on board the launch. He very kindly invited us to go to his bungalow, so we packed a few necessities and went along with him in his car. On the way he told us what had happened.

Some Communists had been arrested and tried for looting; they had been sentenced to a term of imprisonment by the local magistrate, who was a Burman. Thereupon a horde of Communists had besieged the Magistrate and the

Police Officer in their adjoining offices with an ultimatum that they would be kept there without food and water till they released the prisoners. This, of course, they refused to do so the siege began.

Mr Mustill's bungalow was only a few hundred yards from the Magistrate's office. He and his wife were the only Europeans in Katha and they had been in considerable danger. All that day the Communist mob howled and shouted menaces. Mr Mustill thought it quite possible that his house might be attacked. He managed to send a message to Myitkyian to Mr Murray of the Burma Civil Service asking for help to be sent immediately.

That night Mr and Mrs Mustill sat up, not daring to go to bed, while the mob demonstrated and yelled outside the office. Towards dawn the Communists quietened down, many of them falling asleep. The Burmese Magistrate and the Police Officer seized the opportunity and, climbing through a window at the back, they escaped.

Next morning Mr Mustill was thankful to see Mr Murray arrive with an armed police force. The officer in charge of the police had previously served for five years in the French Foreign Legion, and was on special duty chasing bands of *dacoits* through the jungles of Northern Burma. He restored the situation with the speed and efficiency one would expect of the Foreign Legion.

The police surrounded the Communists, who were still in and around the office, and demanded their surrender. As the Chief of the Communists refused to surrender, tear gas was pumped into the office forcing the men to come out. To prevent his men giving themselves up their chief barred the way with a gun and shot two of them dead before he himself was captured.

It was at this moment that we had arrived. In case of further trouble the few Europeans stayed together in Mr Mustill's house. There were only two bedrooms, one of which I shared with Mrs Mustill; the three men were in the other.

In the war the house had been used as a Geisha house by the Japanese. The small window of the pay-box was still to be seen in the verandah. In the garden were the graves of several Japanese officers, including that of a General.

The night passed quietly. Next day we saw a Communist procession taking the bodies of the men who had been killed to the cemetery; it was feared that this might lead to more trouble but, much to our relief, beyond a good deal of shouting and yelling, nothing more happened. I admired very much the way that Mr Murray and Mr Mustill had handled the situation. They showed no fear, walking about unarmed and unguarded.

In the evenings and at night it was bitterly cold in Katha. I slept on the lilo and found it extremely chilly. To warm the sitting-room we had a charcoal brazier, which was very comforting, but the fumes poisoned me badly.

I should have liked very much to visit Myitkyina, but Bill could only take me up the river as far as Moda. On our return journey we glided downstream with the current at a great pace. We tied up at Thabeikkyim for the night. Here we were presented with a wild goose, which the Burmese boy cooked very well for our dinner. This boy had been with Bill before the war, and had only left him when Bill walked out of Burma over the mountains. Bill had given him his gun to keep for him, but he had not been able to hide it from the Japanese, who had taken it from him. He had also hidden all Bill's belongings in a shrine, where for a long time they had been undiscovered, but at the end of the war Chinese troops had found the boxes and looted everything.

Before I left Burma, Bill took me to the lovely hill station of Maymyo, then almost deserted. One felt an impending doom over the whole country. When one thought of the

terrible sufferings of our gallant soldiers who had fought to
save Burma, and of those who had given their lives, and of
others maimed and broken in health for ever, it seemed
tragic that this once happy country should now be torn
asunder with internal strife, and that its rulers were only
anxious to be rid of the British as soon as possible.
European officials were worried about their future, indeed,
it was only a year before their fears were realized and they
all had to leave; a bitter blow for many of them, especially
those with young families.

I left Mandalay by train on 26th January; there was only
one first-class carriage which I had to share with a Jewish
business man. I did not much care for the idea of spending
the night with him alone, but there was no alternative. A
few days later this very train was attacked by Communists
and many of its passengers killed. Bill's timing had been
good.

When I sailed from Rangoon, I stood on deck and
watched the wonderful golden Shwe Dagon Pagoda fade
into the distance, and I wondered what the fate of Burma
would be.

# CHAPTER EIGHTEEN

## *North Borneo*

WHEN I left Burma in January 1947 it was obvious that British rule there would soon come to an end, and indeed it barely lasted another year. As Bill loved the country it was a bitter blow to him to have to leave and give up his career after 14 years of service. To officials with families it was more than a bitter blow, it was a tragedy. Most Forest Officers found jobs, either in timber firms or in the Forest Service of other countries, but it was hard for them to be transplanted when their roots had sunk deeply into the soil of Burma, where they knew and understood the people and spoke their language. Bill spoke Burmese perfectly, also Kachin and several other dialects; all now of very little use to him.

After a long leave Bill was appointed by the Colonial Forest Service to a post in Sarawak, that interesting country in Borneo, which will always be connected with the name of Brooke. This family of pioneers ruled the country for more than 100 years, and brought it from a state of anarchy and chaos to be a well-ordered and prosperous state, now one of the colonies of Britain.

Bill invited me to pay him a visit. In December 1954 I flew to Singapore by B.O.A.C., and after two days there, I went on by Malayan Airways to Borneo. I was eager to see this exciting island of which I had heard blood-curdling tales of pirates, head-hunters and unexplored forests.

Borneo, larger than France, is the third largest island in the world. It is 850 miles long and 600 miles broad. The centre of the island is broken hilly highland with isolated mountains. The plains, chiefly swamps, extend inland 10 to 30 miles from the coast. There are many rivers and Borneo is probably the best watered island in the world. Sinbad, the sailor, is fabled to have visited Borneo. Chinese had already settled on the island in 1206; Chinese coins dating back to 600 B.C. have been found at Santubong, near Kuching. About two-thirds of the island, the southern and eastern portions, is now Indonesia. The British part consists of Sarawak along the West coast, the small state of Brunei, under British protection, and North Borneo, the northern portion.

I alighted at Labuan, a tiny island off the coast of Borneo, under the rule of North Borneo. Here Bill met me, and we engaged rooms at the Airport Hotel, intending to stay one night only. Bill had got two weeks' leave; he had booked berths on M.V. *Kimanis*, sailing next day round the coast of North Borneo. Owing to gales and floods the *Kimanis* was a day late. I was exhausted after the long air journey, and was quite glad of a rest. The R.A.F. have a station at Labuan, the airport is also used by Australian Qantas planes going to Singapore. From the large airy lounge of the hotel we looked over a garden, gay with bright coloured bougainvilleas, to the deep blue sea beyond and the pale blue outline of the coast of North Borneo.

It was hot, but a strong breeze made it quite pleasant. After tea, when it was cooler, we walked across the island to see the War Graves cemetery. It is the last resting place of British and Australian soldiers who fought in the 1939-45 War. The ground is beautifully kept. At the entrance there is a double colonnade joined at one end by a third colonnade to make three sides of a square. The pillars are of red brick; on each pillar is a bronze tablet on which are engraved the names of all the soldiers who died in Borneo who have no known grave. At the foot of the pillars there are flowering shrubs and plants. Round the top of the colonnade is this inscription:

"Hereon are recorded the names of officers and men of the British Commonwealth of Nations who died within and around Borneo during the 1939-45 War and whose graves are known only to God"

There are 1,726 names.

Outside are the actual graves of 2,178 soldiers; 929 British, 1,166 Australian, 1 New Zealander and 82 Indian. Each grave is marked by a small raised block of cement, about a foot square, with a bronze tablet on top, on which is recorded the name, regiment and age of each soldier, with sometimes an epitaph. Between the graves the grass is kept nicely mown, and there are many beautiful flowering shrubs, such as oleanders, hibiscus and bougainvilleas. On the edge of the cemetery grow tulip trees, which have brilliant scarlet flowers all the year round, also many other flowering trees and creepers.

As I looked at the many graves my eyes filled with tears, and I could have wept for the tragedy of these brave men, many of them very young. I thought of the hardships and tortures they had endured at the hand of a cruel enemy, and the agonies they must have suffered before they died. Some of them came from the terrible prisoner camp at Sandakan. Just before the end of the war the Japanese had 2,000 prisoners in this camp at Sandakan. These men had been infamously treated, and the Japanese, realizing that the prisoners would reveal the atrocities perpetrated on them, resolved to get rid of them. They forced them to march across Borneo from East to West through malarious jungles. The men were starving and ill with dysentery and other diseases, but they were driven on mercilessly, till one by one they fell and died. Only four out of the two thousand survived and they did so because they managed to escape and were befriended by natives. The rest perished under conditions of extreme suffering and horror. The march is known as "The March of Death."

Not long ago a Commission was sent from Australia to make inquiries, and reward those natives, who had done anything to help the prisoners. I met Mr Falconar, who had helped on the Commission. He said many and dreadful were the tales he heard. One old woman of 80 had done all she could by giving the prisoners a little food, a drink of water, and a few cigarettes as they staggered by her hut. One must remember that she risked death by doing so. She told of one batch of 20 men, tortured beyond endurance with hunger, disease and fatigue, who lined themselves up by a bank and asked the Japanese to shoot them, which they did. Mr Falconar thought they had found and rewarded all who had had compassion on the unhappy men.

We boarded the M.V. *Kimanis* late at night in a deluge of rain. She is a peculiar looking ship, but a very comfortable one. She sails from Singapore, calling at the ports of Sarawak and North Borneo. She carries about 30 first-class passengers, also some second-class and deck passengers, and a mixed cargo. Her crew is made up of Malays and Chinese; the captain and some of the officers are European.

There were many nationalities on board, including a party of Ibans from Sarawak who were on their way to work in a timber camp near Sandakan. They are small men with long hair, which makes them look rather effeminate, the last thing they really are. Less than a century ago their ancestors were inveterate pirates (hence the old but inaccurate name of Sea Dyaks) and head-hunters. Nowadays they amuse themselves with cock-fighting. Once when Bill was staying in an Iban house far up-river he took a photograph of the headman holding two of his most treasured possessions, a photograph of the Royal Family (a group including King George VI, Queen Elizabeth, Princess Elizabeth, the Duke of Edinburgh and Princess Margaret)

*Plate 9*
Felling a forest giant with primitive tools and methods in tropical evergreen jungle of Borneo. When felled, the extraction is still a problem.

with only 2,226 sq. miles, the present State of Brunei. By a
curious accident of geology, this small area included
(unknown, of course, to the Sultan), hidden beneath a strip
of swampy coastal jungle near the mouth of the River
Belait, the richest oil field in the whole British Commonwealth, first discovered in the 1920s. Thanks to the revenues
from this oil, Brunei has developed rapidly in recent years
into a rich and progressive state, regaining once more
much of the glory and the reputation it enjoyed in Magellan's
day. For the name "Borneo" is only a corruption of
"Brunei."

The festival of the year for Malays is known as "Hari
Raya" and celebrates the end of the month-long Moslem
fast, during which no food or drink may be taken between
sunrise and sunset. The festival lasts for several days,
during which the Malays spend the time visiting the houses
of their friends, where they are entertained with cakes,
sweetmeats, and drinks. Government officers are expected
to visit the houses of Malays in their staff, and in return they
invite the Malays to their own house on Christmas Day or
New Year's Eve. As we had been away at Jesselton for
Christmas Day, Bill invited his forest staff to a *saté* party on
New Year's Eve. A *saté* is a strip of meat (beef or buffalo
as a rule) stuck on a skewer and grilled over a charcoal fire.
The host must allow 70 or 80 *satés* per guest. It is accompanied by a highly spiced soup into which the *satés* are
dipped, cucumber, onion, bread in small cubes, and nuts of
various kinds. I tried a few but found them very tough.

Bill has an office at Kuala Belait on the coast 70 miles
south of Brunei. He had some business to do there, so we
set off early one morning in his Austin Champ. The road
goes over a low range of hills through scrub forest, broken
by an occasional village set among rice fields, for 35 miles,
and then comes to an abrupt end by the sea-shore. We
drove over a sandbank on to the strand, and for the next

N

25 miles we ran along the beach between the waves on one side and a fine belt of *casuarina* trees on the other. Sometimes we splashed through a small stream running out to join the sea, but two or three streams were too deep for us. To cross these we had to ascend a sandbank on to a very rough track leading to a wooden bridge, and then struggle over another track on to the beach again. Bill's Austin Champ with its four-wheel drive managed this easily, but I would not like to attempt it in an ordinary car.

Presently we came to the Tutong river which is of considerable size and has no bridge, we had therefore to cross by ferry, consisting of a lighter towed by a launch. The lighter took one large lorry and a jeep besides our Champ. As we were towed downstream for a mile, and then across to the other bank, Bill and I sat at the back of the lighter with our feet almost in the water, keeping a sharp lookout for crocodiles, but we saw none although it looked a likely place for them.

A few miles farther on we came to the Seria oilfield with its many flares of orange flame, and its miles of enormous pipes, some going right out into the sea to wells 10,000 feet deep. Over 400 Europeans work at Seria, some British, some Australian, and some Dutch. During the war the Japanese worked the wells but, fortunately, when they left they only destroyed the town, leaving the wells unharmed. It is amazing to see what has been done since 1945. A large town has sprung up with hundreds of houses of different grades for the various degrees of labour. The best houses, costing £12,000 each, are occupied by the senior staff. There is a hospital with several doctors, nurses and dentists, a street of good shops, where cold stores arrive every week in huge refrigerator vans, in fact, everything is done by the Shell Company to make life as easy as possible in this tropical climate. There are tennis courts, golf links, hockey grounds, and, of course, a cinema.

The beach, which is a fine one, is spoiled for bathing by the oil in the water, and the debris, which lies about everywhere. Broken bottles, rusty pipes and huge logs are an eyesore as well as being a positive danger. A boy, who cut his foot on a rusty pipe, died of blood poisoning within two days. The logs reminded me of the beaches round Vancouver, where tons and tons of timber lie around, and no one seems to care, or want it.

To reach Kuala Belait, a few miles further south, we drove right through Seria, which was a most interesting experience. Kuala Belait is a small village, where the Brunei Forest Department has an office. We stayed in the Government Rest House, where Bill and I shared a room; it was rather scruffy, but might have been much worse. At any rate it did have a wash-room with a basin, a shower and a pull-plug.

Next day we returned to Brunei by the same route. I found it very hot in the Champ; the heat, rising from under the floorboard, grilled my legs to a frazzle. We stuck in one of the small streams, which Bill took rather fast, making a bow wave, which wet our sparking plugs. I looked anxiously at the sea, and saw that the tide was coming in fast, and would soon reach us. The small stream was getting deeper every moment. Bill and his driver took out the plugs, and cleaned them in feverish haste, finishing the job just in time for our four-wheel drive to get us out.

One day in Brunei we were invited to a Malay wedding. The son of one of the Ministers, quite a boy, was marrying a girl of 15. The European community of Brunei, and the leading Malays and Chinese assembled at the Minister's house. We sat around, some in a small drawing-room, others in the garden, eating cakes and drinking tea. The Malay servants, who handed round trays of cakes, wore gorgeous sarongs of brilliant colours, brocaded into beautiful patterns with threads of real silver and gold; their shirts and trousers were of vivid coloured satins to match, or contrast, with the sarongs. As they rushed to and fro they made a dazzling picture. Brunei brocades, woven locally, are famous, and very costly. When tea was over we were each given an egg wrapped up in coloured paper suspended from a bunch of paper flowers. I did not understand the significance of this.

We were then taken to see the bridegroom being dressed. He was sitting on a stool clad in a plain white shirt and white trousers, surrounded by elders, who proceeded to dress him while the Sultan supervised. First the white shirt was removed, and replaced by a very elegant one of satin. The bridegroom then began to take off his trousers, but was stopped by the Sultan (perhaps owing to the presence of ladies), and the new trousers were put over the old ones. Next a tie, already tied, was slipped over his head, and pulled into place. Then a coat, rather like a naval coat, was donned, and a regal-looking cap. The finished effect, apart from the shirt, resembled a naval uniform.

When the bridegroom was ready, a band of tambourines beat out a rhythm while he went downstairs, and got into a car for the drive to the bride's house. We all followed in cars, and found her seated on a throne in a large drawing-room. She did not look up, appearing to be drugged, which was the part she had to play. The bridegroom took his seat beside her, and his suitcase was put down in front of them signifying that he had come to stay. An elder then placed his hands on the heads of the pair, muttered a few words, and they were married. During the ceremony the bride never once looked up, and later, when she shook hands with the guests, her hand had to be lifted each time.

In the room was a large bed, beautifully decorated with silk hangings and flowers. That night, and for the next three nights, a sort of game is played for the bridegroom may not sleep with his bride, she escapes him every time; if it is a

Royal wedding this game goes on for 40 nights. On the fifth night a curtain is drawn round the bed, and the elders sit outside while the marriage is consummated. This done a sheet is thrown out to show that the bride was a virgin.

About 2 miles downstream from Brunei, the remains of an ancient town are being excavated by the Archaeological Department. One evening we walked there to meet Mr Tom Harrison, D.S.O., who is Curator of the Musuem in Kuching. Lying about everywhere we saw small bits of Ming pottery, and we examined trenches, which revealed the wooden piles of ancient houses. Mr Harrison thinks that the fifth Sultan of Brunei, Sultan Bolkiah, famous in Malay legends throughout the East as Nakoda Ragam, a renowned sea-rover and conqueror, lived here in the 15th century. Jungle has invaded the town, and now not a trace remains above ground of the homes of about 100,000 people. This was the estimate of the population given by the Spaniard Pigafetta, who visited the island in 1521. The excavation work has only just begun, so there is every hope that many things of interest may be found.

# CHAPTER TWENTY

## *Sarawak*

A<small>T THE</small> time of my visit the Brunei airstrip could only accommodate light planes, but was being extended to take Dakotas. When Bill had to attend a conference in Kuching early in February we flew to Labuan in a De Havilland Rapide, the smallest plane I have ever been in. The flight only takes 20 minutes, mostly over the sea. At Labuan we changed into a Dakota of Malayan Airways.

As we flew over Sarawak, we looked down on a country of vast forests and swamps. Long rivers, dark chocolate in colour, wind and wriggle their way through the forests, looking from the air like great writhing snakes. There are no roads in these tracts, the only means of communication being along the rivers or by air. Towards the interior could be seen endless ranges of densely-forested hills, going up to 5,000 or 6,000 feet (the highest mountain in Sarawak, Mt. Murud 7,950 ft., was not visible). Following the coast we saw beaches of golden sand fringed with palm trees.

Sarawak is inhabited by several different tribes:

1. *Ibans* (formerly known as Sea Dyaks), about 200,000, are basically hill paddy farmers, but their aggressive and war-like character led them into piracy and head-hunting forays, which caused frequent armed clashes with the Brooke Government. Since the Emergency started in Malaya their thirst for adventure has been put to good use by employing them as trackers and soldiers in the war against the bandits. Not only have they earned several awards for gallantry, including one George Cross, but their

198

extrovert and friendly nature has endeared them to many British officers and men with whom they have served in the field. At home they live in longhouses, like several of the other indigenous peoples of Borneo. The longhouse probably evolved for security reasons during the head-hunting days, and consists of a number of families, usually 10 to 30, living under one roof. Each family is responsible for building its own segment of the house, consisting of a room (for cooking, eating, and sleeping) at the back, and a covered passage and verandah in front, with an open platform outside on which the paddy is dried in the sun. Farming of hill paddy, by shifting cultivation, is carried on by each family independently; if a family requires any help on a farm, it has to be paid for either in cash or on a labour exchange basis.

Touring in Sarawak is very different from what I knew in India. Instead of elephants and strings of camels, the Forest Officer has a dug-out and an outboard engine (there are more outboard engines per head of population than anywhere else in the world); away from the main towns and district headquarters there are no rest-houses—it is the custom for touring officers to stay in longhouses.

2. The *Chinese*, also about 200,000, are the chief traders, rubber and pepper planters, and smallholders. They are shrewd business men, expert gardeners, hard workers, and thrifty. They tend to have enormous families, and have increased greatly in numbers during the present century. One old Chinese farmer told me he had 96 grandchildren, and was astonished when I said I had only two. He took me to see his pepper growing; the vine is trained up wooden posts, and has to be heavily manured and carefully tended.

3. The *Malays*, about 100,000, all adherents of the Islam religion, are one of the most charming and courteous people in the world, and take life more easily than the Chinese. Because they were better educated than the other indigenous peoples, and live mainly in or near the larger

towns, they have always formed the backbone of the Government services (Police, Customs, Forests, etc.).

4. The *Land Dyaks*, also about 100,000, live in the hills of south-western Sarawak. They have almost nothing in common with the Ibans or "Sea Dyaks"—even the language is entirely different—and the confusion has arisen from the fact that in the old days the word "Dyak" was used for almost any person living in Borneo who was not a Malay or Chinese.

5. The *Melanaus*, about 35,000, grow sago in the coastal swamps of central Sarawak. The sago is obtained from the pith of the sago palm and is exported for use as industrial starch—only a small part of the total exported is made into sago puddings for schoolboys.

6. The *Kayans*, *Kenyahs*, and *Kelabits*, not much more than 10,000 in all, live in northern Sarawak, but there are a lot more over in Indonesian Borneo. They live in longhouses like the Ibans, and tattoo the body extensively. The women distend the lobes of the ears, which they weigh down with heavy ear-rings till they touch the shoulders; it must be a very painful process, and looks weird to our Western eyes.

7. The *Muruts* live in the most northerly district of Sarawak, and most of them have turned to Christianity in recent years.

8. The *Penans* are the most primitive people in the island. They grow no crops but rely entirely on wild sago and on what they can shoot with their beautifully-made blowpipes. They are jungle nomads, moving from one sago patch to another (the wild sago comes from a different species of palm, smaller than the cultivated sago of the Melanaus).

A number of other tribes are recognized by anthropologists, but numerically they are unimportant.

On a broad view Sarawak is one enormous forest; 75 per cent. of the country is virgin tropical rain forest, and another 10 to 15 per cent. is secondary bush subject to

Touring in Sarawak. Bill dragging his camp up a stream.

*Plate 12*

*Plate 13 A*

A Kayan chief. Note the tattooing which is widely practised among the Kayans of Northern Sarawak. The ear ornament is the canine tooth of a leopard cat.

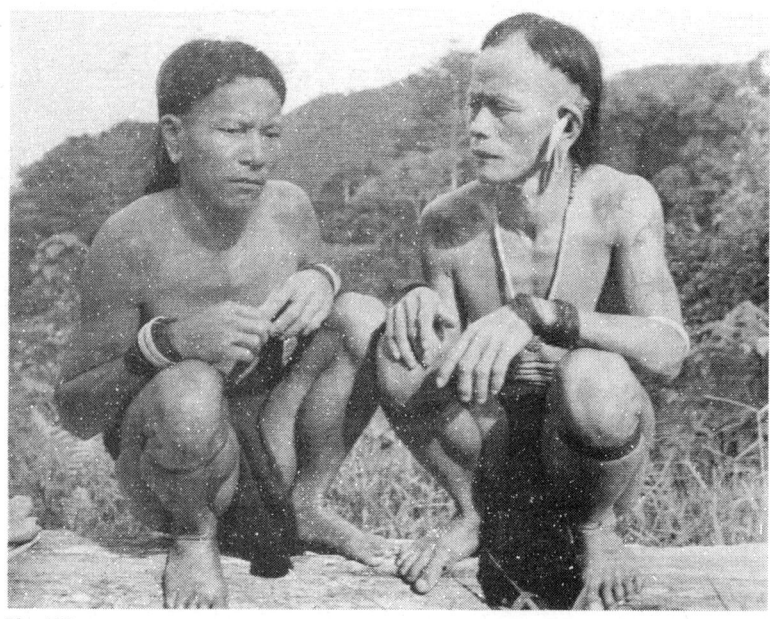

*Plate13B*

Two Kayans at their longhouse. The women distend the lobes of their ears which they weigh down with heavy ear-rings.

shifting cultivation, on which enough paddy is grown almost to supply the country's needs. Although there is a vast amount of wood in the country, the difficulties of getting it out are such that only a comparatively small area of the forest is commercially workable for timber. Since the war timber has become an important export, notably to the British Isles, but it is overshadowed by the product of an artificial forest created by man—the forest of the rubber trees. The rubber tree is remarkably adaptable—not only has it been successfully transplanted half-way round the world from its home in the forests of the Amazon, but also it will grow on any sort of soil from dry hillsides to wet peat-swamps. Most of Sarawak's revenue derives from the export duties on rubber, and her prosperity rises and falls with the price of rubber on the world markets. Pepper and sago are other exports of importance. A windfall (in the literal sense) is the crop of illipe nuts, which occurs on the average once in four or five years. These nuts are the fruits of forest trees belonging to the same genus as the *sal* tree of northern India; they contain an edible fat which is used by chocolate manufacturers as an alternative to cocoa butter. The fallen nuts are gathered by the Ibans, dried, and the kernels brought down to the nearest market for sale. In an "illipe nut year" the revenue from the export duty on kernels may exceed 1,000,000 dollars. It is interesting to reflect, when eating a chocolate, that part of it may have come from the top of a forest giant in the interior of Borneo.

When James Brooke was made Rajah of Sarawak in 1841 he set himself three tasks:

(i) to relieve the unfortunate Land Dyaks from oppression;
(ii) to suppress piracy;
(iii) to abolish head-hunting.

He was strong and brave and he had a natural gift for

managing the wild tribes, but his difficulties were enormous. At times he almost gave up in despair. The British Government, instead of helping him, did everything in their power to obstruct him, even going so far as to help his enemies, men who had murdered Englishmen in his employ. It is incredible, but it is true.

As Rajah, James Brooke did not attempt to set up a new constitution; all that was necessary was to enforce the existing laws fairly, and modify the penalties where necessary. Taxation was collected honestly, where before people had been wickedly robbed. Soon the tribes realized that they could get justice, and confidence in the Government was inspired. The poor Land Dyaks, who had fled to the mountains and jungles, came out of their hiding. News soon spread that Sarawak was the one spot in Borneo where they would not be persecuted so they settled down happily; thus James Brooke gained his first objective.

Head-hunting, being an ancient tribal custom, could not be suppressed all at once. A young man could not win a bride till he had proved his valour by presenting her with a head; it did not matter what sort of head, it might be of a man, woman or child. When a chief died his warriors had to get several heads so that his spirit might be properly attended in his new life. A Dyak once said to a European, "You like books, we like heads."

Rajah Brooke promised to protect all tribes in his raj. Every murder was punished, so that in time head-hunting grew less, but outside his jurisdiction it went on for many years.

A bitter struggle was waged against the pirates, who were cunning and cruel. They would descend on a coast, attack a village, sack and burn it, kill the defenders, carry away men, women and children as slaves, slaughter the cattle, and ravage the plantations. The wretched captives would be herded together at the bottom of the pirates' boats in appalling conditions. Those who survived were sold as slaves on another island. If the pirates were pursued they would kill all the captives, and throw them overboard.

.James Brooke went out against the pirates on many occasions, defeated them and burned their boats, but, after lying low for a time, the pirates built other vessels, and renewed their attacks. In 1849 the pirates were stronger than ever, they even sent a message to the Rajah taunting him to come out against them. Not a day passed without news reaching Kuching of some village burned, or some vessels captured. Refugees streamed into Kuching from villages that had been sacked. The Rajah wrote, "No news except of Dyaks, and rumours of Dyaks, Dyaks here, Dyaks there, and Dyaks everywhere."

Something had to be done. Admiral Sir Francis Collier arrived off Kuching in H.M.S. *Albatross*, and with him James Brooke made plans to give the pirates a final blow, which was delivered at the battle of Beting Maru, August 1849. The pirates were utterly routed; they lost 300 killed, and 500 died of wounds and exposure.

Thus the Rajah had accomplished his three aims, but his troubles were not at an end. In 1857 there was a Chinese rising in Kuching organized by a Secret Society. The Rajah had been warned, but took no heed. Suddenly in the middle of the night hordes of Chinese, armed to the teeth, swarmed into the Government buildings and stockades. Charles Plenty, the Rajah's steward, gives the following account:

I was sleeping in a room near the Raja, who had not been well for some days. The attack took place about midnight with fearful yelling and firing. I hurried out of bed, and met the Raja in the passage in the dark who, at the moment, took me for one of the rebels, grabbed me by the throat, and was about to shoot me, when he fortunately discovered it was me. We then opened the venetian window of my room, and saw poor Mr Nicholetts murdered before our eyes. The Raja said, "Ah, Plenty, it will be our turn next." Then we went to another part of the house, where the crowd of rebels was even thicker. The Raja seemed determined to fight. While he was loading a double-barrel gun for my use, our light went out, and he had to do without. The Raja then led the way to his bathroom, under his bedroom, and rushed out of the door. The rebels, having gathered round Mr Nicholett's body, left the way pretty clear, and the Raja, with his sword and revolver in hand, made his way to a small creek, and swam under the bow of a boat that had brought the rebels. Being unable to swim, I ran up the plantation and rushed into the jungle. The Raja's beautiful house was blazing from end to end, and the light reflected for a great distance. Mr Crookshank's and Mr Middleton's houses were also burning. At daybreak I heard Malay voices; they, like myself, were running away from the town, which was in the hands of the rebels. They kindly clothed me and took me to the Raja.

The Rajah escaped by swimming across the creek, he then joined some Malays, and with them organized the escape of the surviving women and children to a spot farther up the coast. How barbarous the Chinese had been in their attack is told by Mr St. John:

When the rebels burst into Mr Middleton's house, he fled, and his wife following found herself in the bathroom, and by the shouts was convinced that her retreat was cut off. In the meantime the Chinese had seized her two children, and brought the eldest into the bathroom to show the way his father had escaped. Mrs Middleton's only refuge was a large waterjar; there she heard the poor little boy questioned, pleading for his life, and heard his shriek when the fatal sword was raised which severed his head from his body. The fiends kicked the little head with loud laughter from one to another. They then set fire to the house, and she distinctly heard the second child shrieking as they tossed him in the 'flames. Mrs Middleton remained in the jar till the falling embers forced her to leave. She then got into a neighbouring pond, and thus escaped the eyes of the Chinese.

The Chinese, hearing that the Rajah's nephews were coming to his aid with a large force, decided to retreat with their plunder. They were hotly pursued by the furious Malays and Dyaks, who harried them on either side, as they went through the jungle on their way to the frontier, killing any stragglers, till very few of the rebels reached Dutch Borneo. Kuching was in ruins, and the Government was bankrupt. The British Government refused any aid, and the Rajah, in his despair, had thoughts of inviting the help of a foreign Government, but he bravely struggled on alone, and with the help of his loyal subjects the country gradually recovered.

It will be realized that Rajah Brooke's life was full of difficulties and dangers. That he succeeded in turning Sarawak from a nest of pirates and head-hunters to a peaceful well-ruled country is of eternal credit to him. He is one of the greatest of all British pioneers, and had he had the co-operation of the British Government he would have been able to accomplish even more. To the Rajah's unaided efforts, frowned upon at home, England owes it that Sarawak, Brunei and Labuan are not now parts of Indonesia, and had his policy not been discredited, Siam, the Sulu archipelago, and the whole of New Guinea might now have been under British influence. The last of the three white Rajahs, Sir Vyner Brooke, ceded Sarawak to the Crown in 1946, when it became a Crown Colony.

It took us two hours to fly the length of Sarawak, a journey that must have taken many days in the time of Rajah Brooke. As I looked down on the vast forests and the isolated villages I realized something of the enormous task James Brooke had had, and I marvelled at his tenacity and courage.

The airport is several miles from Kuching. We were met by Dr Brunig, a German, who had recently joined the Forest Department. He drove us at a furious speed over a flooded and appalling road to Kuching. To reach his house we had to leave the car and cross the River Sarawak, 100 yards wide, in a Government sampan with an out-board motor. Tied up at the quay was the *Rajah Brooke*, a small steamer, which sails between Kuching and Singapore once a fortnight. On the opposite bank we saw the Astana (palace), formerly Rajah Brooke's residence and now Government House. We landed and went on in a Government bus to Dr Brunig's bungalow on the outskirts of the town. It had a delightful situation with a magnificent view to the hills beyond. To the north, Mount Santubong is the dominant feature, its jagged cliffs showing up a deep violet; to the west, ranges of hills rise to the Indonesian border.

One morning I visited the large and busy bazaar, where the shops are mostly owned by Chinese. Beautiful brocades, silks, and hand-woven damasks can be bought, but what took my fancy was an enormous Dyak hat, made of coloured straw artistically decorated with beads. As it would have been an unwieldy addition to my luggage, I could not buy it.

Our five days in Kuching were soon over. Bill and I flew to Singapore on our way to Kepong, Selangor, where Bill had work awaiting him.

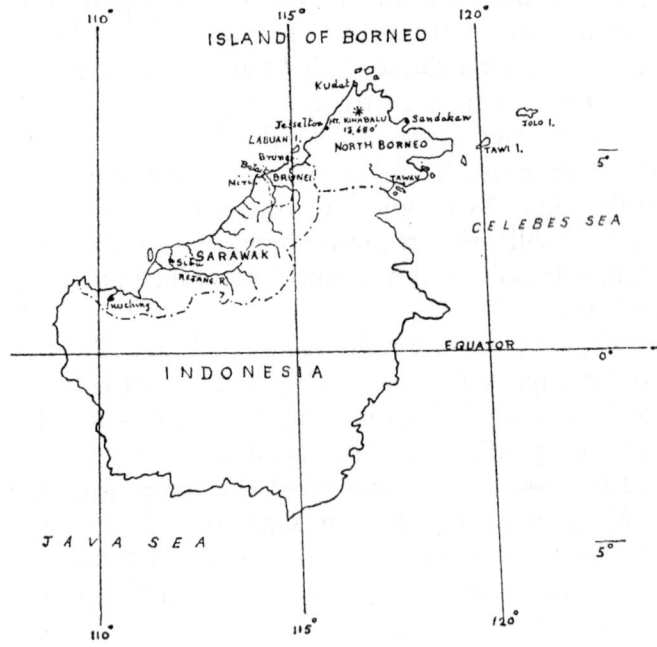

# CHAPTER TWENTY-ONE

# *Kepong*

THE flight from Kuching to Singapore takes 3½ hours, and is, of course, over the sea nearly all the way. As we circled over the harbour before landing, we had a good view of it and the outlying islands.

Hotels in Singapore are extremely expensive. My room for one night, with no meals included, came to £4 10s. od. The next night we went on the narrow gauge line to Kuala Lumpur, 250 miles north of Singapore. We had a most luxurious compartment in the air-conditioned coach, and enjoyed an excellent dinner in the dining-car. I noticed a sentry with fixed bayonet on every coach. As we rumbled through the forest I thought of the bandits, who were still giving so much trouble, especially in the State of Johore, through which we were passing. Next morning we reached Kuala Lumpur, where we were met by Mr Wyatt-Smith, a Forest Officer working at the Forest Research Institute at Kepong, about 10 miles from Kuala Lumpur. We stayed with him and his wife in their delightful bungalow on the slopes of a hill with a magnificent view of the mountains, which run down the centre of the Malay Peninsula. Behind the bungalow there is dense forest, in front to the south-east, there rises a ridge of high hills, where it was thought that the bandit chief had his stronghold, and where he kept his printing press. If we had only known where to look, we could probably, with field-glasses, have seen the very place.

No one seemed to worry much about the bandits, and, of course, the emergency was much less severe than it had been

some months before. The Wyatt-Smiths told us that earlier
on the authorities had wanted to sandbag their bungalow
up to the roof, but, as it would have made the house
stiflingly hot, they had not had it done, preferring to risk a
stray bullet. Everyone kept fierce dogs, and there were
large electric lamps at the corners of the house, which lit up
all round it at night. The bandits did not worry Forest
Officers, their objectives were the Police, the Military,
rubber planters and tin miners. The Wyatt-Smiths told us
that several of their planter friends had been killed. A
lorry belonging to the Forest Department was ambushed
one day, and three of its occupants killed, for which act the
bandits sent an apology, saying the lorry had been mistaken
for a police lorry.

There is an amusing true story of a Hospital Sister, who
was driving along a jungle road in her uniform. She saw a
lorry by the side of the road, and noticed some legs sticking
out at the back. As she went past, British soldiers in the
lorry fired a volley at some bandits, who were clearly
visible down a bank. The Sister drove on raising her right
hand as she went by; afterwards she said she did not know
why she had raised her hand. The British soldiers and the
bandits were taken by surprise, and both sides watched her,
not a shot was fired. One British soldier remarked, "Blimey,
it is as good as a film show." Asked why she had gone on,
and not turned back, the Sister replied that she could not
have done that as there was no room to turn, and she did
not know how to reverse! The legs she had seen at the back
of the lorry were those of three men who had been killed in
the ambush.

Several times I saw helicopters going over to bomb sus-
pected bandit camps on the hills beyond, and we often saw
detachments of soldiers returning from searching the
jungles.

One day we went over the Leper Settlement at Sungei

*Plate 14*

A typical Iban longhouse on the edge of a stream, in the depths of the endless virgin tropical rain forest of Sarawak.

Buloh, which was then under the care of Dr Molesworth. The Settlement covers an area inside a perimeter of 6 miles, and it contains over 2,000 lepers. The whole place is run on ultra modern lines, and I was very struck and surprised at the cheerfulness of most of the patients.

First of all we visited the nurseries for babies, who are taken away from their mothers at birth, and kept in the nurseries for six months. The first room contained 14 babies of under two months, one born only that morning. Each child has a nice little cot, covered with a mosquito-net at night. If allowed to remain with their mothers these babies would undoubtedly develop leprosy, but they are born free of it. There were two other rooms for older babies nearly all of them Chinese or Malays. After six months the babies are either adopted, or they are taken care of by some relation. The mothers may only see them once a month.

We next visited the schools and classes of different standards, girls and boys being taught together. They were all nicely dressed, the girls in blue gym dresses with white blouses, the boys in blue shorts and white shirts. At first sight there did not seem to be anything wrong with the children, but, if one looked more closely, one noticed blotches on some of their faces, or some disfigurement, such as a nose half-eaten away, or a bandaged arm, or leg. I did not like to stare even though the children are not self-conscious; they all seemed to be very happy and cheerful. The highest class was doing Cambridge Higher Certificate. The schools are run on a self-help basis; the boys work in the garden, the girls do the washing and mending. Many of the teachers are patients, and they are enthusiastic about their work.

We went on to see the dormitories. There are about 50 beds in each long airy room. The beds are just planks covered with white sheets, but these are used normally in Chinese houses. Each child has a locker for itself, and there

o

are pictures on the walls, many of them of Queen Elizabeth and the Royal Family. The rooms were gay with paper streamers and flowers, the aftermath of decorations put up for Chinese New Year.

Leaving the dormitories we made our way through a leper village, where a patient can have a house, and live there with his family, if they are also lepers. Each house has a small vegetable garden and a few banana trees. Rations are provided every day, and there is a shop where extras can be bought. Patients can earn money if they are tradesmen such as carpenters, bricklayers, etc., for the maintenance work of the Settlement is done, as far as possible, by patients. We visited one workshop, where artificial limbs were made, a great many of them being needed in the Settlement.

The hospital has a European matron, who warned me before we went in that we should see some sad and terrible sights. One poor lad of about 15 had had his leg amputated that morning, the look on his face was tragic, and I felt desperately sorry for him. On another bed was a terribly disfigured woman leper, who was also mentally defective, and looked hardly human. The hospital was the only part of the Settlement where I saw a look of despair on the faces of the lepers.

We were walking down a long covered passage when we heard a great commotion, and saw a small crowd staring at a man on the roof of an outhouse. This man, a leper and also a lunatic, had escaped from the room where he had been locked up and had managed to climb on to the roof. He was shouting, and was busily tearing up the tiles, which he flung down, so that it was dangerous to go too near. Down crashed one tile after another to an accompaniment of yells. This continued for about 15 minutes, the holes in the roof gaping wider and wider. The maniac then seemed to tire, for he produced a cigarette and began to smoke. One of the doctors approached as near as he dared, and asked why he was behaving like this, to which the maniac replied that he was not given enough to eat, and he also had other grievances he wanted to talk about to the head doctor. He was told that no one could talk to him while he was on the roof, but if he came down his complaints would be looked into. For a few minutes he continued to smoke, then he climbed down quite quietly. It was amazing what an amount of damage he had done in so short a time.

Of recent years great strides have been made in the treatment of leprosy. Leprosy is no longer hopeless and incurable, for patients can be completely cured if the disease has not progressed too far, and they can take up life in the outside world again. Those who come in too late to be completely cured, can lead a happy life in the Settlement. Some of those, who have been cured, are so happy in the Settlement that they do not want to leave it.

We visited the kitchens, which are equipped with great electrically-heated cauldrons for boiling rice and every modern device, and from there we went to see the playing-fields, where Girl Guides were having a meeting. The Settlement must seem like heaven to the poor lepers, who in former times lived as outcasts and beggars.

Dr Molesworth, like Bill, is a keen ornithologist, so he arranged for us to go bird watching in the jungles behind the Settlement. We each had a pair of binoculars, and we crept in single file along paths through the tropical forest. The jungle is so thick that it is difficult to see the birds at all, and how Bill can recognize what kind they are as they flash past, I cannot understand. I could hardly see the bird, let alone whether it had a white feather under its eye or tail! It was very damp underfoot, in fact, the whole place was dripping wet. Beautiful ferns carpeted the ground, and giant creepers festooned the trees. Several times we heard wild pigs dash off as we approached, and once, to my great excitement, we heard an argus pheasant call. Bill in all his years in the forest has only seen one once. We watched a troupe of monkeys swinging about from tree to tree, and we saw pugs of a *sambar*. A very occasional tiger visits these forests, but they are rarely seen. Compared to the forests I knew so well in India, which teemed with wild life, these forests are empty of game.

We all had on rubber shoes, and we made as little noise as possible as we wandered down the narrow paths. I came last in the line, which is a dangerous place when walking through tropical forests infested with leeches, but I forgot about it at the time, and walked on happily.

We went back to Dr Molesworth's house for tea. I was sitting on a cretonne-covered chair, when I noticed that Mrs Molesworth was gazing at the carpet under my feet. Looking down I saw that both my legs were pouring blood on to the cretonne and the carpet, making an awful mess. I then saw a repulsive fat leech drop off one leg, and there were five others attached to me in various places, one right up on my thigh. The rest of the party seemed to think it was a huge joke, but I was not amused. I went up to the bathroom, and got the leeches off by applying salt to them; I was dripping blood everywhere, and it was some time before I could staunch it with cottonwool and sticking-plaster. I went home looking as if I had been in a battle.

The Templer Park is about 22 miles from Kuala Lumpur. It can hardly be described as a game reserve as there are very few wild animals in the area, which is a bowl-shaped valley surrounded by hills with a massive limestone rock of 300 feet in the centre. The Park is more one for pleasant walks through the jungle, along sylvan paths by small streams of clear water; it has not the wild appeal of the Hailey Park, described in Chapter Eleven, which teems with jungle animals, and where tigers roam about on the roads quite boldly even in daytime.

*Plate 15*

A pepper garden, Tarat Agricultural station 34 miles from Kuching. The hop-looking plants on the left are pepper. In the foreground a banana leaf.

On our return to Singapore we met Mr Loke Wan Tho, famous for his wonderful bird photographs. He and Bill were discussing the book Bill is writing on the birds of Borneo. Bill's first book, *Birds of Burma*, is considered to be a masterpiece. Many copies of the first edition were destroyed in the war, so that the remaining ones became scarce and valuable.

My wonderful tour was at an end. I said goodbye to Bill at the airport, and watched his plane take off for Borneo and Brunei. I had no time to feel sad as my own plane, a Qantas, left almost immediately for Ceylon and England.

# *Index*

# Index

217

# THE MOUNTED TROOPS OF
# THE BRITISH ARMY
## 1066–1945
### By COLONEL H. C. B. ROGERS, o.b.e.

Author of *The Pageant of Heraldry*
*Royal 8vo.* 42s. *nett*
With many plates in full colour and black and white

The greater part of a book about the horse soldier must, of necessity, be devoted to the cavalryman for it was not until the eighteenth century that there was any other mounted arm.

Association with horses seemed to produce a type of individual who was to be found in all units of the Army where "stables" formed part of the day's routine. He was a simple soul, slow of speech and movement (when dismounted), and inclined to some richness of language. When reasonably contented he grumbled incessantly and especially when engaged in the care of the horses he loved. Mechanisation seems to have found no place for him. At any rate he has gone; and the Army is the poorer for his departure.

This is the history of his service from the days when the Normans brought the war horse to England, till garages replaced stables in the military barracks. It deals with his uniform and equipment, his weapons and horses and his life in peace and war. No attempt has been made to describe campaigns or battles, except to provide such background as is required to show the conditions under which the horse soldier fought and the methods he used.

# MODEL SOLDIERS

By JOHN G. GARRATT

*Profusely illustrated in colour and Black & White*

*Royal octavo.* 42s. *nett*

During the last thirty years or so a growing interest has been observed in children's playthings, both for their intrinsic and often artistic value, and also as a delightful aspect of social history. After many years of neglect they are being assiduously collected, and researches are being made into their origins. To those who, in their childhood, played with lead soldiers, or who today purchase them for their children, it may come as a surprise to know that the history of these little figures goes back to the time of the ancient Egyptians, and that throughout the succeeding centuries they have been the most popular of all playthings for boys.

It is only within comparatively recent times that a serious attempt has been made to collect specimens and to record them for posterity. The Frenchmen D'Allemagne and Forrer were probably the first to realize their historical significance, and their example was so speedily followed that today there is a vast and world-wide body of collectors, all interested in the sometimes complex, and always fascinating history of the subject.

In the present comprehensive volume the history of military and other miniatures is traced from the earliest times through the Middle Ages and the subsequent periods of famous and much sought after masters of the art. Makers in almost every country are thoroughly classified and all that is known of their methods is recorded.

Considerable attention is paid to the modification and adaptation of existing commercial figures for special purposes or for uniforms or actions not otherwise attainable. Much attention is paid also to the actual casting or modelling of figures by the keen amateur collector, and to the building and arrangement of dioramas.

There is a great wealth of coloured illustrations and photographs, and the text is not only concisely arranged for reference purposes, but is itself well documented with contemporary drawings.